United States Government Accountability Office

GAO

Report to the Congress

I0469275

June 2011

RECOVERY ACT

Funds Supported Many Water Projects, and Federal and State Monitoring Shows Few Compliance Problems

GAO
Accountability ★ Integrity ★ Reliability

GAO-11-608

June 2011

RECOVERY ACT

Funds Supported Many Water Projects, and Federal and State Monitoring Shows Few Compliance Problems

GAO
Accountability · Integrity · Reliability

Highlights

Highlights of GAO-11-608, a report to the Congress

Why GAO Did This Study

The American Recovery and Reinvestment Act of 2009 (Recovery Act) provided $4 billion for the Environmental Protection Agency's (EPA) Clean Water State Revolving Fund (SRF) and $2 billion for the agency's Drinking Water SRF.

The Recovery Act requires GAO to review funds made available under the act and comment on recipients' reports of jobs created and retained. These jobs are reported as full-time equivalent (FTE) positions on a Web site created for the Recovery Act on www.Recovery.gov.

GAO examined the (1) status and use of Recovery Act SRF program funds nationwide and in nine states; (2) EPA and state actions to monitor the act's SRF program funds; (3) EPA and selected states' approaches to ensure data quality, including for jobs reported by recipients of the act's funds; and (4) challenges, if any, that states have faced in implementing the act's requirements.

For this work, GAO, among other things, obtained and analyzed EPA nationwide data on the status of Recovery Act clean and drinking water funds and projects and information from a nonprobability sample of nine states that represent all but 1 of EPA's 10 regions. GAO also interviewed EPA and state officials on their experiences with the Recovery Act SRF program funds.

GAO is making no recommendations in this report, which was provided to EPA for its review and comment. EPA did not comment on the report.

View GAO-11-608 or key components. For more information, contact David C. Trimble at (202) 512-3841 or trimbled@gao.gov.

What GAO Found

The 50 states have awarded and obligated the almost $6 billion in Clean Water and Drinking Water SRF program funds provided under the Recovery Act, and EPA indicated that all 50 states met the act's requirement to award funds to projects under contract 1 year after the act's passage. States used the funds to support more than 3,000 water quality projects, and according to EPA data, the majority of the funds were used for sewage treatment infrastructure and drinking water treatment and distribution systems. Since the act was passed, states have drawn down almost 80 percent of the SRF program funds provided under the act. According to EPA data, states met the act's requirements that at least (1) 20 percent of the funds be used to support "green" projects and (2) 50 percent of the funds be provided as additional subsidies. In the nine states GAO reviewed, the act's funds paid for 419 infrastructure projects that helped address major water quality problems, but state officials said in some cases the act's requirements changed their priorities for ranking projects or the projects selected. In addition, although not required by the act, the nine states used about a quarter of the funds they received to pay for projects in economically disadvantaged communities, most in additional subsidies.

EPA, states, and state or private auditors took actions to monitor Recovery Act SRF program funds. For example, EPA officials reviewed all 50 states' Recovery Act SRF programs at least once and found that states were largely complying with the act's requirements. Also, in part as a response to a GAO recommendation, in June 2010 EPA updated—and is largely following—its oversight plan, which describes monitoring actions for the SRF programs. Furthermore, state officials visited sites to monitor Recovery Act projects, as indicated in the plan, and found few problems.

Officials at EPA and in the nine states have also regularly checked the quality of data on Recovery.gov and stated that the quality has remained relatively stable, although GAO identified minor inconsistencies in the FTE data that states reported. Overall, the 50 states reported that the Recovery Act SRF programs funded an increasing number of FTE positions for the quarter ending December 2009 through the quarter ending June 2010, from about 6,000 FTEs to 15,000 FTEs. As projects were completed and funds spent, these FTEs had declined to about 6,000 FTEs for the quarter ending March 2011.

Some state officials GAO interviewed identified challenges in implementing the Recovery Act's Clean and Drinking Water SRF requirements for green projects and additional subsidies, both of which were continued with some variation, in the fiscal year 2010 and 2011 appropriations for the SRF programs. Officials in four states said achieving the green-funding goal was difficult, with one suggesting that the 20 percent target be changed. In addition, officials in two of the four states, as well as in two other states, noted that when monies are not repaid into revolving funds to generate future revenue for these funds, the SRF program purpose changes from primarily providing loans for investments in water infrastructure to providing grants.

_____ **United States Government Accountability Office**

Contents

Abbreviations

CBR	Clean Water Benefits Reporting
EPA	Environmental Protection Agency
FTE	full-time equivalent
OIG	Office of Inspector General
OMB	Office of Management and Budget
PBR	Program Benefits Reporting
Recovery Act	American Recovery and Reinvestment Act of 2009
SRF	State Revolving Fund

United States Government Accountability Office
Washington, DC 20548

June 29, 2011

Report to the Congress

In response to the serious economic crisis that began in 2007, Congress enacted the American Recovery and Reinvestment Act of 2009 (Recovery Act).[1] Among other things, the purposes of the Recovery Act were to preserve and create jobs, promote national economic recovery, and provide long-term economic benefits through infrastructure investments, including water infrastructure.[2] In past reports, GAO has identified the need for stimulus funds to be timely, targeted, and temporary.[3] To this end, Recovery Act funds were directed to support services and build infrastructure in a wide range of areas, including health, education, transportation, energy, and water. In particular, the Recovery Act provided $6 billion for the Environmental Protection Agency's (EPA) Clean Water and Drinking Water State Revolving Fund (SRF) programs. These funds represented a significant federal investment in the nation's water infrastructure at a time when, according to a 2010 Congressional Budget Office report, overall spending on infrastructure has been declining, and when reported problems with the quality and safety of water supplies have raised questions about the condition of the nation's infrastructure.[4]

The Recovery Act mandates that GAO conduct bimonthly reviews of the funds used by states and determine whether the act is achieving its stated purposes.[5] The Recovery Act also requires GAO to comment and report quarterly on, among other things, estimates of job creation and retention, counted as full-time equivalent (FTE), as reported by recipients of

---

[1] Pub. L. No. 111-5, 123 Stat. 115.

[2] As of June 3, 2011, the Department of the Treasury had paid out $217.5 billion in Recovery Act funds for use by states and localities. For updates, see http://gao.gov/recovery.

[3] GAO, *Physical Infrastructure: Challenges and Investment Options for the Nation's Infrastructure*, GAO-08-763T (Washington D.C.: May 8, 2008).

[4] Congressional Budget Office, *Public Spending on Transportation and Water Infrastructure* (Washington, D.C., November 2010).

[5] Pub. L. No. 111-5, § 901(a)(1).

Recovery Act funds.[6] In this report, we update our May 2010 report and add new information on the use of Recovery Act funds provided for the Clean and Drinking Water SRF programs.[7] Specifically, for this report we examined the (1) status and use of Clean and Drinking Water Recovery Act SRF program funds nationwide and in selected states; (2) actions taken by federal, state, and other agencies to monitor and ensure accountability of these program funds; (3) approaches federal agencies and selected states have taken to ensure data quality, including data for jobs reported by recipients of these program funds; and (4) challenges, if any, that states have faced in implementing Recovery Act requirements for the Clean and Drinking Water SRF programs.

To address these objectives we obtained and analyzed nationwide data from EPA on the status of Recovery Act Clean and Drinking Water SRF program funds and projects, as well as information from selected states on their use of Recovery Act funds. We discussed this information and Recovery Act requirements and reporting with EPA and state officials, including program officials in state environmental and public health departments responsible for the SRF programs and state Recovery Act officials. To develop a more in-depth view of the states' use of Recovery Act funds for Clean and Drinking Water SRF programs, we selected a nonprobability sample of nine states that we had not reviewed in our previous bimonthly reports, representing all but 1 of EPA's 10 regions.[8] For these states, we obtained and analyzed information on the states' prioritization processes for the programs, the amount of Recovery Act

---

[6]Pub. L. No. 111-5 § 1512(e). FTE data provide insight into the use and impact of the Recovery Act funds, but recipient reports cover only direct jobs funded by the Recovery Act. These reports do not include the employment impact on suppliers (indirect jobs) or on the local community (induced jobs). Both data reported by recipients and other macroeconomic data and methods are necessary to understand the overall employment effects of the Recovery Act.

[7]This month we are also reporting on the status and use of Recovery Act funds for transportation programs. See GAO, *Recovery Act: Funding Used For Transportation Infrastructure Projects, but Some Requirements Proved Challenging*, GAO-11-600 (Washington, D.C.: June 29, 2011). We last reported on the use of Recovery Act Clean and Drinking Water SRF program funds for water in GAO, *Recovery Act: States' and Localities' Uses of Funds and Actions Needed to Address Implementation Challenges and Bolster Accountability*, GAO-10-604 (Washington, D.C.: May 26, 2010).

[8]These states were Alabama, Connecticut, Maryland, Michigan, Missouri, New Mexico, Nevada, Washington State, and Wyoming. We did not select any states in EPA Region 2— which includes New Jersey, New York, and Puerto Rico—because we had reviewed New Jersey and New York in previous Recovery Act reports.

funds provided to projects, the amount of funding provided to green projects and additional subsidies, the amount of funds received and spent, and the FTEs funded for each project and in total. For data gathered from the nine states, we had state officials review, verify, and correct, when necessary, data in EPA's Recovery Act databases; we found the data sufficiently reliable for our purposes. We also obtained and analyzed national data from EPA on award amounts, funds drawn down by states, categories of water infrastructure projects funded, and FTEs.[9] We used these data to assess the reliability of Recovery.gov data reported by the states and determined that the data were reliable for our purposes. Appendix I discusses our scope and methodology in more detail.

Our oversight of programs funded by the Recovery Act has resulted in more than 100 related products with numerous recommendations since we began reporting on the Recovery Act.[10] This report updates agency actions in response to recommendations from previous bimonthly and recipient reporting reviews that have not been fully implemented (referred to as open recommendations) in appendix II.

We testified in May 2011 on our preliminary observations concerning this work, and this report provides our final results. We conducted this performance audit from September 2010 through June 2011, in accordance with generally accepted government auditing standards. Those standards require that we plan and perform the audit to obtain sufficient, appropriate evidence to provide a reasonable basis for our findings and conclusions based on our audit objectives. We believe that the evidence obtained provides a reasonable basis for our findings and conclusions based on our audit objectives.

Background

Both the Clean Water and Drinking Water SRF programs authorize EPA to provide states and local communities with independent and sustainable sources of financial assistance. This assistance is typically in the form of low- or no-interest loans, for projects that protect or improve water quality and that are needed to comply with federal drinking water regulations and protect public health. Repayment of these loans replenishes the funds and

---

[9]In addition to our analyses of EPA recipient report data, we continued, as in prior rounds, to perform edit checks and analyses on all prime recipient reports to assess data logic and consistency and identify unusual or atypical data.

[10]See http://gao.gov/recovery for related GAO products.

provides the ability to fund future loans for additional projects. The Clean Water SRF program was established in 1987 under the Clean Water Act, which was enacted to protect surface waters, such as rivers, lakes, and coastal areas, and to maintain and restore the physical, chemical, and biological integrity of these waters. The Drinking Water SRF program was established in 1996 under the Safe Drinking Water Act, which was enacted to establish national enforceable standards for drinking water quality and to guarantee that water suppliers monitor water to ensure compliance with standards.

The Recovery Act provided $6 billion for EPA's Clean Water and Drinking Water SRF programs.[11] This amount represents a significant increase over the federal funds awarded to the non-Recovery Act, or base, SRF programs in recent years. From fiscal years 2000 through 2009, annual appropriations averaged about $1.1 billion for the Clean Water SRF program and about $833 million for the Drinking Water SRF program. In addition to increasing funds, the Recovery Act included some new requirements for the SRF programs. First, projects funded with Recovery Act SRF program funds had to be under contract—ready to proceed—within 1 year of the act's passage, or by February 17, 2010. Second, states had to use at least 20 percent of these funds as a "green reserve" to provide assistance for green infrastructure projects, water- or energy-efficiency improvements, or other environmentally innovative activities. Third, states had to use at least 50 percent of Recovery Act funds to provide "additional subsidies" for projects in the form of principal forgiveness, grants, or negative interest loans.[12] Uses for these additional subsidies can include helping economically disadvantaged communities build water projects, although these uses are not a requirement of the act.

---

[11]The $6 billion in Recovery Act funds includes about $39 million in Clean Water Act Section 604(b) Water Quality Management Planning Grants. Section 604(b) of the Clean Water Act requires the reservation each fiscal year of a small portion of each state's Clean Water SRF allotment—usually 1 percent—to carry out planning under Sections 205(j) and 303(e) of the Clean Water Act. States generally use 604(b) grants to fund regional comprehensive water quality management planning activities to improve local water quality. In addition, the $6 billion includes a small amount of funding for trust territories, tribal governments, and the District of Columbia. Any reference to Recovery Act funds in this report excludes these water quality planning, territorial, tribal, and District of Columbia funds.

[12]These are loans for which the rate of interest is such that the total payments over the life of the loans are less than the principal of the loans. In contrast to these additional subsidies, financial assistance typically replenishes funds and provides the ability to fund future loans for additional projects.

With some variation, Congress incorporated two of these requirements—green projects and additional subsidies—into the fiscal year 2010 and 2011 base SRF program appropriations.

In addition to meeting requirements from program-specific provisions, water projects receiving Recovery Act funds have to meet requirements from the act's Buy American and Davis-Bacon provisions. The Recovery Act generally requires that all of the iron, steel, and manufactured goods used in a project be produced in the United States, subject to certain exceptions.[13] Federal agencies can issue waivers for certain projects under specified conditions, for example, if using American-made goods is inconsistent with the public interest or if the cost of goods is unreasonable; the act limits the "unreasonable cost" exception to those instances when inclusion of American-made iron, steel, or other manufactured goods will increase the overall project cost by more than 25 percent. Furthermore, recipients do not need to use American-made goods if they are not sufficiently available or not of satisfactory quality. In addition, the Recovery Act applies Davis-Bacon provisions to all Recovery Act-funded projects, requiring contractors and subcontractors to pay all laborers and mechanics at least the prevailing wage rates in the local area where they are employed, as determined by the Secretary of Labor.[14] Contractors are required to pay these workers weekly and submit weekly certified payroll records.

To enhance transparency and accountability over Recovery Act funds, Congress and the administration built numerous provisions into the act, including a requirement that recipients of Recovery Act funding—including state and local governments, private companies, educational institutions, nonprofits, and other private organizations—report quarterly on a number of measures. (Recipients, in turn, may award Recovery Act funds to subrecipients, which are nonfederal entities.) These reports are referred to as "recipient reports," which the recipients provide through one Web site, www.federalreporting.gov (Federalreporting.gov) for final publication through a second Web site, www.recovery.gov (Recovery.gov). Recipient reporting is overseen by the responsible federal agencies, such as EPA, in accordance with Recovery Act guidance provided by the Office of Management and Budget (OMB). Under this guidance, the federal agencies are required to conduct data quality checks of recipient data, and

---

[13]Pub. L. No. 111-5, § 1605.

[14]Pub. L. No. 111-5, §1606.

recipients can correct the data, before they are made available on Recovery.gov. Furthermore, additional corrections can be made during a continuous correction cycle after the data are released on Recovery.gov.

A significant aspect of accountability for Recovery Act funds is oversight of spending. According to the federal standards of internal control, oversight should provide managers with current information on expenditures to detect problems and proactively manage risks associated with unusual spending patterns.[15] In guidance issued in February 2009, OMB required each federal agency to develop a plan detailing the specific activities—including monitoring activities—that it would undertake to manage Recovery Act funds. EPA issued its first version of this plan in May 2009, as required, and updated this document as OMB issued new guidance.[16]

All Recovery Act SRF Program Funds Have Been Awarded and Obligated, and with Some Exceptions, States Reported Supporting Major Infrastructure Projects and Helping Economically Disadvantaged Communities

Nationwide, the 50 states have awarded and obligated the almost $6 billion in Clean Water and Drinking Water SRF program funds provided under the Recovery Act and reported using the majority of these funds for sewage treatment infrastructure and drinking water treatment and distribution systems, according to EPA data. In the nine states we reviewed, the states used these funds to pay for infrastructure projects that help to address major water quality problems, although state officials said that in some cases, Recovery Act requirements changed their priorities or the projects selected for funding. The nine states also used their Recovery Act funding to help economically disadvantaged communities, but state officials indicated that they continue to have difficulty helping these communities.

---

[15]GAO, *Standards for Internal Control in the Federal Government*, GAO/AIMD-00-21.3.1 (Washington, D.C.: November 1999).

[16]The most recent version of the plan is EPA, *Environmental Protection Agency Recovery Act Plan: A Strong Economy and a Clean Environment* (Washington, D.C., June 1, 2010).

Nationwide, EPA Data Indicate States Awarded and Obligated the Majority of Recovery Act Water Funds for Sewage Treatment Infrastructure and Drinking Water Treatment and Distribution Systems

As of March 30, 2011, states had awarded funds for contracts and obligated the $4 billion in Clean Water SRF program funds and $2 billion in Drinking Water SRF program funds provided under the Recovery Act.

Requirement to Award Recovery Act Funds to Projects under Contract within 1 Year

As we reported in May 2010, EPA indicated that all 50 states met the Recovery Act requirement to award Recovery Act funds to projects under contract by February 17, 2010, 1 year after the enactment of the Recovery Act.[17] In the 2 years since the Recovery Act was passed, states have drawn down from the Treasury approximately 79 percent, or $3.1 billion, of the Clean Water SRF program funds and approximately 83 percent, or $1.7 billion, of the Drinking Water SRF program funds.[18]

Across the nation, the states have used the almost $6 billion in Recovery Act Clean and Drinking Water SRF program funds to support more than 3,000 water quality infrastructure projects. As shown in figure 1, the states used the majority of their Recovery Act Clean Water SRF program funds to improve secondary and advanced treatment at wastewater treatment plants,[19] as well as projects to prevent or mitigate sanitary sewer overflow.[20]

---

[17]GAO-10-604.

[18]The states draw down funds from the Treasury to reimburse contractors for work already conducted on projects.

[19]Wastewater treatment involves several processes, including primary treatment to remove suspended solids; secondary treatment to further remove contaminants using biological processes; and tertiary or advanced treatment to remove additional material in wastewater, such as nutrients or toxic chemicals.

[20]Sanitary sewer overflows can occur as a result of inclement weather and can pose significant public health and pollution problems, according to EPA.

Figure 1: Categories of Clean Water SRF Projects Funded by the Recovery Act in 50 States

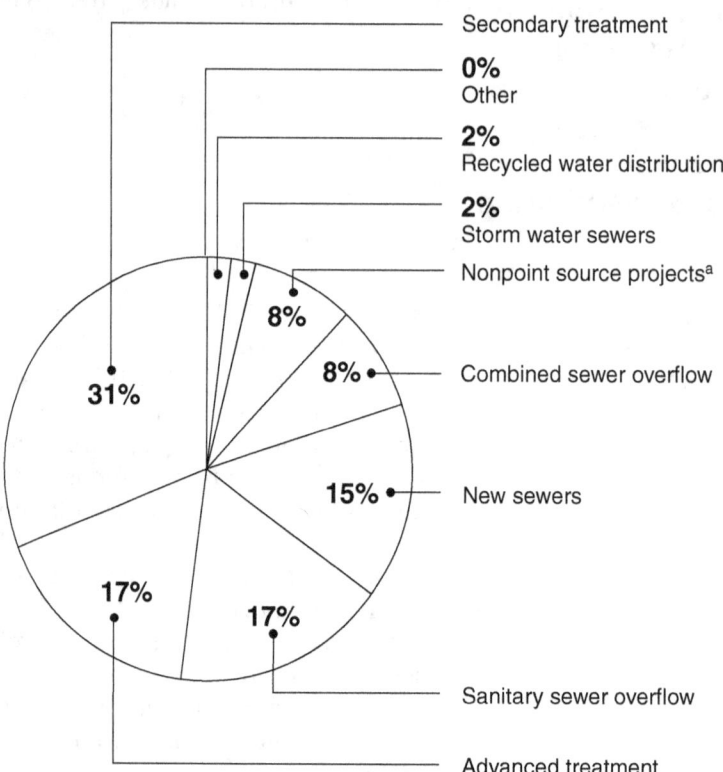

Secondary treatment

0%
Other

2%
Recycled water distribution

2%
Storm water sewers

Nonpoint source projects[a]

8%

8% — Combined sewer overflow

31%

15% — New sewers

17%

17%

Sanitary sewer overflow

Advanced treatment

Source: GAO analysis of EPA data.

[a]Nonpoint source projects are intended to address nonpoint source pollution—which refers to water pollutants from nonpoint sources. These are diffuse sources from a variety of land-based activities, such as timber harvesting, agriculture, and urban development.

In Montevallo, Alabama, for example, the state provided Clean Water SRF program funds to upgrade an outdated wastewater treatment plant in Shelby County that served a population of about 5,000. The upgrade added two large settlement basins to hold and treat wastewater, replacing a series of small basins (see fig. 2). The additional treatment is expected to remove nutrients, such as nitrogen and phosphorus, to help the county meet higher standards in the nearby waterways receiving the plant's discharged water.

Figure 2: Old and New Settlement Basins at Montevallo, Alabama, Wastewater Treatment Plant

Old settlement basin

New settlement basin under construction

Source: GAO.

As shown in figure 3, the states used about half of their Recovery Act Drinking Water SRF program funds to construct projects to transmit and distribute drinking water, including pumps and pipelines to deliver water to customers. States used about 40 percent of their funds for projects to treat and store drinking water.

Figure 3: Categories of Drinking Water SRF Projects Funded by the Recovery Act in 50 States

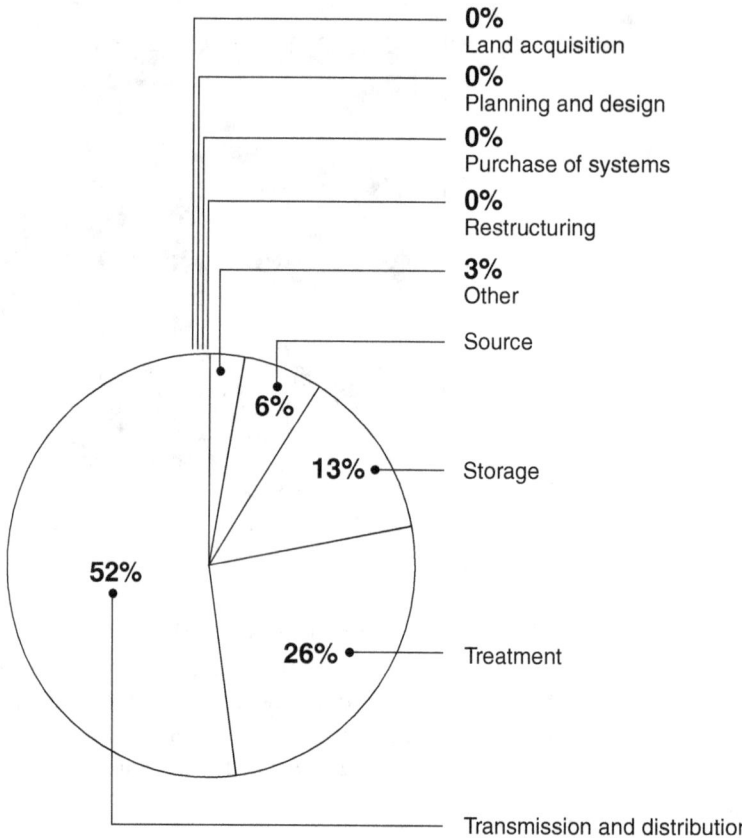

0% Land acquisition

0% Planning and design

0% Purchase of systems

0% Restructuring

3% Other

Source

6%

13% Storage

52%

26% Treatment

Transmission and distribution

Source: GAO analysis of EPA data.

In Baltimore, Maryland, for example, the state provided funds to the city to cover one of its treated water reservoirs at the Montebello drinking water treatment plant. Before it was covered, the reservoir was open to birds and other sources of contamination, and city water managers used a mesh-like material to try to keep birds from landing on or using the water. When the project is complete, the reservoir will be a huge, cement tank buried under soil and vegetation (see fig. 4 for the project under construction in December 2010).

Figure 4: Montebello Drinking Water Treatment Plant, Treated Water Reservoir under Construction, December 2010

Montebello Plant 2

Water reservoir under construction and before being covered with soil and vegetation

Source: GAO.

Requirement to Use at Least 20 Percent of Funding for Green Projects

According to EPA data, all states met the requirement to use at least 20 percent of their Recovery Act funding for green projects, with $1.1 billion of total Clean Water SRF program funds going to green projects and $544 million of total Drinking Water SRF program funds going to green projects. According to EPA, the goal of supporting green projects is to promote green infrastructure, energy or water efficiency, and innovative ways to sustainably manage water resources. Green infrastructure refers to a variety of technologies or practices—such as green roofs, porous pavement, and rain gardens—that use or mimic natural systems to enhance overall environmental quality. In addition to retaining rainfall and snowmelt and allowing them to seep into groundwater, these technologies can mitigate urban heat islands,[21] and sequester carbon. Figure 5 shows the amount of Clean Water and Drinking Water SRF program funds that states awarded to green projects by type of project.

---

[21]Urban heat islands are metropolitan areas that are significantly warmer than the surrounding rural areas.

GAO-11-608 Recovery Act

Figure 5: Total Recovery Act Funds Awarded to the 50 States for Green Projects under the Clean Water and Drinking Water SRF Programs, by Type of Project

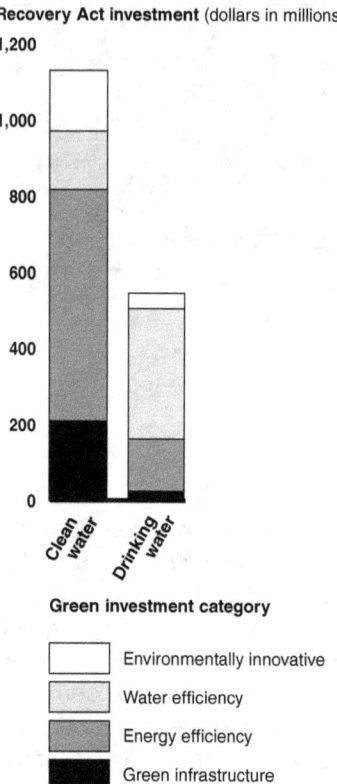

Source: GAO analysis of EPA data.

In Annapolis, Maryland, for example, city officials used Clean Water SRF program funds to construct a green parking lot, a project that helped retain and filter storm water runoff. (See fig. 6.)

Figure 6: Gotts Court Parking Lot Improvements, Annapolis, Maryland

Green parking lot

Source: GAO.

In Los Alamos, New Mexico, city officials used Clean Water SRF program funds to install facilities to recycle water at the city's wastewater treatment plant; the recycled water will be used as washwater—water that is used in the plant to clean equipment (see fig. 7). Because New Mexico is an arid state, the reuse of water saves operating costs for the plant, as well as scarce water resources.

Figure 7: Effluent Washwater System in Los Alamos, New Mexico, Wastewater Treatment Plant

Source: GAO.

Booster pump station building

Requirement to Provide at Least 50 Percent of Funding as Additional Subsidies

Nationwide, the states also met the Recovery Act requirement to provide at least 50 percent of the Clean Water and Drinking Water SRF program funds as additional subsidies in the form of principal forgiveness, negative interest loans, or grants (i.e., not loans to be fully repaid). Of the total Recovery Act funds awarded, 76 percent of Clean Water SRF Recovery Act funds and 70 percent of Drinking Water SRF Recovery Act funds were distributed as additional subsidies. Figure 8 shows the total Clean Water and Drinking Water Recovery Act funds awarded by the states as principal forgiveness, negative interest loans, or grants. The remaining 24 percent of Clean Water SRF Recovery Act funds and 30 percent of Drinking Water SRF Recovery Act funds will be provided as low- or no-interest loans that will recycle back into the programs as subrecipients repay their loans.

Figure 8: Amount of Recovery Act Funds Awarded by the 50 States as Principal Forgiveness, Grants, or Negative Interest Loans and Low- or No-Interest Loans

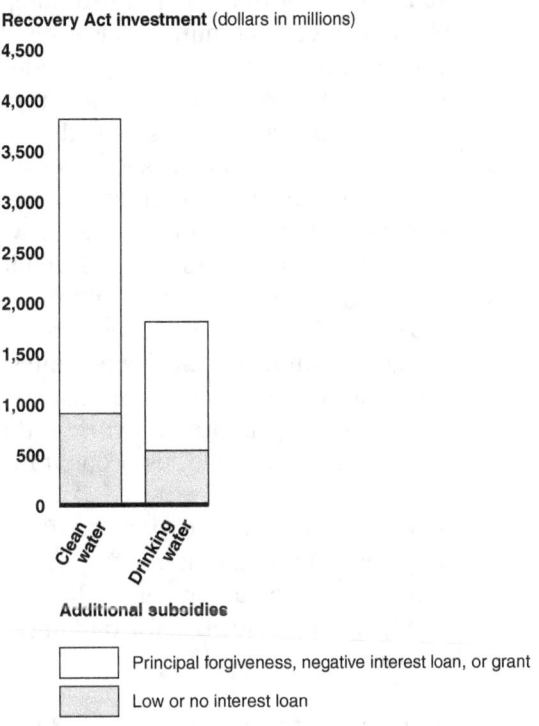

Recovery Act investment (dollars in millions)

Additional subsidies

☐ Principal forgiveness, negative interest loan, or grant
▨ Low or no interest loan

Source: GAO analysis of EPA data.

Recovery Act Water Funds Generally Addressed Major Water Quality Problems in Nine States, although Recovery Act Requirements Changed Some State Priorities or Projects

In the nine states we reviewed, Recovery Act Clean and Drinking Water SRF program funds have been used to address some of the major clean and drinking water problems in the states. These nine states received a total of about $832 million in Recovery Act SRF program funds—about $579 million for their Clean Water SRF programs and about $253 million for their Drinking Water SRF programs. In total, these funds supported 419 clean and drinking water projects.[22]

To award SRF program funds, each of the nine states used a system to score and rank water projects seeking funds to address water quality

---

[22]In our May 2010 report, the 14 states we reviewed distributed more than $2.8 billion in Recovery Act funds among nearly 1,400 water projects through their Clean Water and Drinking Water SRF programs.

problems that were submitted by local municipalities or utilities. The projects with the most points are considered the highest priority on the list of projects for funding. For example, Nevada officials told us that groundwater contamination is their state's major clean water quality problem, which their ranking system addresses by designating the elimination of existing contamination of groundwater as one of the state's highest-scoring priorities. In addition, in most of the nine states we reviewed, compliance is a key aspect of their ranking system, allowing points to be awarded to infrastructure projects that help the states eliminate causes of noncompliance with federal or state water quality standards and permits. Officials in most of the nine states said that they generally obtain information on their water systems' compliance with federal and state water quality standards through discussions with their program compliance staff and from state databases. Michigan, for example, assigns a significant amount of points to clean water projects—such as sewage treatment works—that will help these projects comply with enforcement actions brought by the state against a municipality.

In the nine states we reviewed, officials said that Recovery Act priorities—including the requirements for projects to be ready to proceed to contract 1 year after the passage of the Recovery Act or for green projects—either changed their priorities for ranking and funding projects or changed the projects they funded.

Readiness of a project to proceed to construction requirement. In the nine states, officials included readiness to proceed and other Recovery Act requirements in their ranking system and selected projects on the basis of that ranking system or said that they did not fund—or bypassed—top-ranked projects that were not ready to proceed to construction by February 17, 2010, 1 year after the passage of the Recovery Act. For example, Washington State's two top-ranked clean water projects did not receive Recovery Act SRF program funds because they could not meet the February 2010 deadline. The projects were to decommission septic systems and construct a wastewater treatment plant to reduce phosphorus discharges to the Spokane River. In Wyoming, many of the projects that were not ready to proceed were water treatment plants, which state officials said take longer to design and plan for construction. Although these higher-ranked projects did not receive Recovery Act funds, at least two states were able to fund these projects in other ways, such as through state grants or non-Recovery Act SRF program funds.

Green project requirement. Three states listed green projects separately from other projects. For example, Washington State officials who manage the Clean Water SRF program told us that they established a green projects category because they had anticipated that projects focused primarily on energy and water efficiency (green projects) would not score well under their ranking system, which focuses on water quality protection and improvements. Other states funded green projects ahead of higher-ranked projects. For example, Nevada did not fund a number of higher-ranked projects and funded a lower-ranked drinking water project that had green components. Similarly, Maryland bypassed many projects to fund the first green-ranked project on its list.

Buy American and Davis-Bacon provisions. State officials identified a few projects that did not proceed because potential subrecipients either did not want to meet one or more Recovery Act requirements, such as the Buy American and Davis-Bacon provisions, or did not want to increase the cost of their projects. For example, local officials in Alabama withdrew their application for a drinking water project because the project was already contracted without Buy American and Davis-Bacon wage requirements, and an addendum to the contract to meet the regulations would have increased the project's cost. Similarly, officials in all nine states said that a few communities indicated they preferred to have their projects funded from the base program, or chose not to apply for or withdrew from the Recovery Act funding process to avoid paperwork or the additional costs associated with the act's Buy American or Davis-Bacon requirements.[23] For example, Wyoming officials said that potential subrecipients for three clean water projects refused funding, citing time constraints or difficulty meeting Buy American requirements.

Despite changes in priorities for ranking and funding projects or in the projects funded, officials reported that they were able to fund projects with Recovery Act funds that helped resolve their major water problems. For example,

- Wyoming officials told us that Recovery Act clean and drinking water funds were used to replace aging sewer and water lines, which they said was one of their major problems.

---

[23]Our February 2010 report on the Davis-Bacon provisions of the Recovery Act found that program officials had mixed views on the effect of the provisions on program costs. See GAO, *Recovery Act: Officials' Views Vary on Impacts of Davis-Bacon Act Prevailing Wage Provision*, GAO-10-421 (Washington, D.C.: Feb. 24, 2010).

- Connecticut officials said that Recovery Act funding helped support four combined sewer overflow projects, which resulted in fewer discharges of partially treated sewage into the area waterways.[24]

- Nevada officials told us that Recovery Act funding will help with the rehabilitation and relining of sewer ponds in four rural communities, eliminating groundwater pollution, a major problem in the state.

- Washington State officials who manage the Drinking Water SRF program told us that six of their Recovery Act projects addressed arsenic drinking water contamination, a major water problem in the state.

States Supported Economically Disadvantaged Communities, in Part by Using Additional Subsidies Authorized under the Act, although Officials Cited Continuing Difficulty in Helping These Communities

Although the Recovery Act did not require states to target Clean and Drinking Water SRF program funds to economically disadvantaged communities, six of the nine states that we reviewed distributed more than $123 million in clean water funds, and eight of the nine states distributed almost $78 million in drinking water funds under the SRF Recovery Act programs to these communities.[25] This amount represents about 24 percent of the almost $832 million in Recovery Act funds that the states were awarded.[26] As shown in table 1, a large majority of the funds provided to these communities were provided as additional subsidies—grants, principal forgiveness, and negative interest loans.[27]

[24]These flows can contain untreated human and industrial waste.

[25]States differ in how they define disadvantaged communities. In general, disadvantaged community status takes into account factors such as median household income and community size.

[26]In our May 2010 report, we found that the 14 states in that review provided $1.2 billion, or about 43 percent of total funds, for assistance in disadvantaged communities.

[27]In total, the nine states we reviewed provided more than $558 million of their Recovery Act funds—67 percent—in the form of additional subsidies to all projects. Of this money, 30 percent was awarded to projects in economically disadvantaged communities.

Table 1: Number of Economically Disadvantaged Community Projects Funded for Nine States under the Recovery Act SRF Programs

Dollars in millions

SRF Programs	Number of projects funded	Amount of SRF funds provided to projects	Number of projects funded in economically disadvantaged communities	Amount of SRF funds provided to economically disadvantaged projects	Amount of SRF funds provided to economically disadvantaged projects as additional subsidies	Percent of additional subsidies provided to economically disadvantaged projects
Clean Water	261	$579	70	$123	$101	82%
Drinking Water	158	253	63	78	66	85
Total	419[a]	$832	133	$201	$167	83%

Source: GAO analysis of state-provided data.

[a]All 50 states funded more than 3,000 such projects.

According to officials in five of the nine states we reviewed, their states provided additional subsidies to economically disadvantaged communities because the communities would otherwise have had a difficult time funding projects. For example, New Mexico officials told us that they directed additional drinking water subsidies to economically disadvantaged communities because these communities have historically lacked access to capital. Officials in Nevada told us such communities not only have a difficult time funding projects, they also have some of the projects with the highest priority for addressing public health and environmental protection concerns. In addition, officials in a few other states told us that economically disadvantaged communities often lack the financial means to pay back loans from the SRF programs or lack funds to pay for the upfront costs of planning and designing a project. Officials in at least two states also said that many economically disadvantaged communities lack full-time staff to help manage the water infrastructure.

Even with the additional subsidies available for projects, officials in a few states said that economically disadvantaged communities found it difficult to obtain Recovery Act funds. For example, Missouri officials told us that the Recovery Act deadline was the single most important factor hindering the ability of these communities from receiving funding. New Mexico officials also told us that because these communities typically do not have funds to plan and develop projects, few could meet the deadline, and several projects that sought Recovery Act funds could not be awarded funding owing to the deadline.

We gathered information on economically disadvantaged communities from the nine states we reviewed because EPA did not collect the information. In April 2011, the EPA Office of Inspector General (OIG) reported that EPA could not assess the overall impact of Recovery Act funds on economically disadvantaged communities because the agency did not collect data on the amount of Clean and Drinking Water SRF program funds distributed to these communities nationwide.[28] The OIG recommended that EPA establish a system that can target program funds to its objectives and priorities, such as funding economically disadvantaged communities.

Number of FTEs Have Declined as Most Recovery Act Funds Are Spent

For the quarter ending December 2009 through the quarter ending June 2010, the number of FTEs paid for with Recovery Act SRF program funds increased each reporting quarter, from about 6,000 to 15,000 FTEs for planning, designing, and building water projects (see fig. 9). As projects were completed and funds spent, the number of FTEs funded had declined to about 6,000 for the quarter ending March 2011. Following OMB guidance, states reported on FTEs directly paid for with Recovery Act funding, not the employment impact on suppliers of materials (indirect jobs) or on the local communities (induced jobs). In addition, state officials told us that, although funding varies from project to project, as much as 80 percent of a project's funding generally is used for materials—such as cement for buildings and equipment such as turbines, pumps, and centrifuges—and the remainder pays for labor or FTEs.

---

[28]EPA Office of Inspector General, *Evaluation Report: EPA Faced Multiple Constraints to Targeting Recovery Act Funds*, Report No. 11-R-0208 (Washington, D.C.: Apr. 11, 2011).

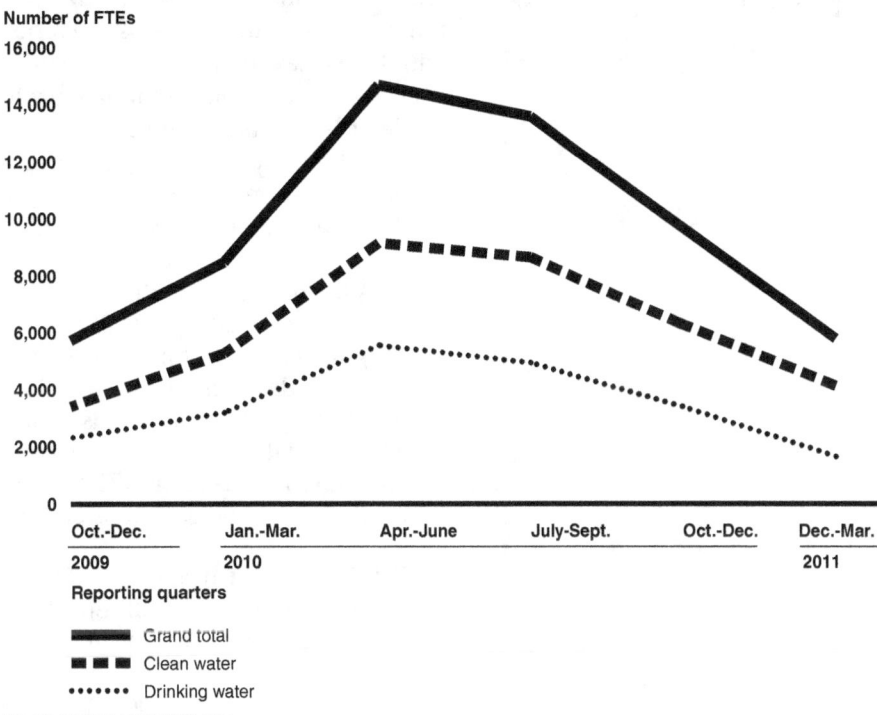

Figure 9: SRF FTEs Reported as Funded with Recovery Act Funds in 50 States from October 2009 through March 2011

Number of FTEs

Reporting quarters

— Grand total
▪ ▪ ▪ Clean water
•••••• Drinking water

Source: GAO analysis of EPA data.

Note: We did not include data from the first reporting quarter because of concerns about comparability. Nearly all recipients reported funding at least a partial FTE with Recovery Act funds. In comparing clean and drinking water funds across the reporting quarters from October 2009 through March 2011, we found that the percentage of recipients who reported funding at least a partial FTE ranged from 97 percent to 100 percent.

EPA, States, and Other Agencies Took Actions to Monitor SRF Program Funds and Found Projects Largely Complied with Recovery Act Requirements

As Recovery Act Clean Water and Drinking Water SRF program funds have been spent over the last 2 years, EPA officials have monitored projects and spending activity and found that states have generally complied with Recovery Act requirements. Similarly, in the nine states we reviewed, state officials indicated that the site visits they made to monitor Recovery Act projects found few problems. Furthermore, state auditors in the nine states we reviewed continue to monitor and oversee the use of Recovery Act funds, and their reports showed few significant findings.

EPA's Monitoring Found That States Largely Complied with Recovery Act Requirements

Since the Recovery Act was enacted, EPA officials have reviewed all 50 states' Recovery Act Clean and Drinking Water SRF programs at least once and have found that states are largely complying with the act's requirements.[29] In our May 2010 report, we recommended that EPA work with the states to implement specific oversight procedures to monitor and ensure subrecipients' compliance with provisions of the Recovery Act-funded Clean Water and Drinking Water SRF programs.[30] EPA updated its oversight plan for Recovery Act funds, in part, as a response to our recommendation. The plan describes the following monitoring actions for the Recovery Act Clean and Drinking Water SRF programs:

- EPA headquarters staff should visit both SRF programs in every region in fiscal years 2010 and 2011, review all states' Clean Water SRF programs and all states' Drinking Water SRF programs for these years, and provide training and technical assistance, as needed. Although the oversight plan recommends headquarters staff visit all regions in 2011, EPA officials decided instead to provide regional training on program eligibility requirements. The officials said that they had visited the regions once and saw greater benefit in providing training.

- EPA's Office of Wastewater Management and Office of Ground Water and Drinking Water will report bimonthly to the Assistant Administrator for Water on oversight activities.

- Regional staff should conduct state reviews twice a year using an EPA-provided checklist or comparable checklist, examine four project files, and conduct four transaction tests, which can be used to test if an internal control is working or if a dollar error has occurred in the processing of a transaction. In addition, regional staff are to discuss each state's inspection process and audit findings with state officials, and update headquarters staff on any findings.

- The regions are to submit to headquarters (1) program evaluation reports, which describe how states are managing their Recovery Act SRF funds and projects; (2) Recovery Act project review checklists, to examine compliance with Recovery Act requirements; and (3)

---

[29]Examples of the issues raised include missing Davis-Bacon or Buy American clauses or paperwork, inappropriate payments, or instances in which paperwork was missing to show that debarment lists had been checked. The reports identified corrective actions that the states planned to take or showed that the issues had been resolved through the review process.

[30]GAO-10-604.

transaction testing forms, to determine if any erroneous payments were made.

- Regional staff should conduct at least one site inspection of a clean water project and a drinking water project in each state each year.

According to our review of the Clean and Drinking Water SRF program evaluation reports for the 50 states, EPA regional officials generally carried out the instructions in EPA's oversight plan. As of June 1, 2011, these officials had visited most state programs twice, although they visited some state programs only once or did not have documentation of the visits. During visits, officials reviewed the files for proper documentation pertaining to Davis-Bacon, Buy American, and green project requirements. Additionally, although not required to do so by the oversight plan, regional officials attempted to visit at least one clean water and one drinking water SRF Recovery Act project in every state each year. Headquarters officials said that the regional staff met this goal for drinking water projects in 2010, but they were not able to visit a clean water project in each state because of time and budget constraints.

EPA headquarters officials said that they oversaw each region's activities by visiting the regional offices to review files on the states. Headquarters officials told us that when they visited regional offices, they checked whether key state documents were maintained in the region's state file, such as the Recovery Act grant application and any accompanying amendments; the state's intended use plan, which details a state's planned use of the funds, including the criteria for ranking projects and a list of ranked projects; and a copy of the grant award and conditions. Furthermore, headquarters officials said that they used a regional review checklist to examine each region's oversight practices by, for example, determining whether the regions received and reviewed states' analyses of costs (business cases) and if the regions ensured that the states updated key reporting data for their Recovery Act projects each quarter. Headquarters officials also said that they briefly reviewed the Drinking Water and Clean Water SRF program evaluation reports when they reviewed the regions' activities. Headquarters officials said they had imposed a 60-day time frame for completing these reports because the regional staff were not submitting the reports in a timely manner.

Additionally, the EPA OIG is conducting performance audits of EPA's and states' use of Recovery Act funds for the Clean and Drinking Water SRF programs and unannounced site inspections of Recovery Act-funded projects. Between May 1, 2010, and May 1, 2011, the OIG has conducted eight unannounced site visits.[31] Six of the eight visits yielded no findings.[32] The OIG issued recommendations for the other two projects:

- In a visit to Long Beach, California, the OIG found that a contractor did not fully comply with federal and state prevailing wage requirements, which resulted in underpayments to employees. The OIG recommended that EPA require the California State Water Resources Control Board to verify that the city is implementing controls to ensure compliance with prevailing wage requirements.[33]

- In a visit to Astoria, Oregon, the OIG found that the city understated the number of FTEs created or retained with Recovery Act funds. In addition, the OIG found that a change order for one of four contracts awarded did not meet applicable procurement requirements. The OIG recommended that EPA Region 10 require the Oregon Department of Environmental Quality to require the city to correct the number of FTEs and report the corrected number to the federal government. The OIG also recommended that the regional administrator of EPA Region 10 require the Oregon Department of Environmental Quality to disallow the costs incurred under the change order unless Astoria was able to show that the costs met applicable Oregon requirements. Officials for EPA, the Oregon Department of Environmental Quality, and the city concurred with the corrective actions.[34]

The Chairman of the Recovery Accountability and Transparency Board testified in June 2011 that there has been a low level of fraud involving Recovery Act funds. He noted that less than half a percent of all reported Recovery Act contracts, grants, and loans had open investigations and only 144 convictions—involving about $1.9 million of total Recovery Act

---

[31]According to the OIG, site visits included a tour of the project, interviews with the subrecipient and contractor personnel, a review of the subrecipient's systems used for reporting purposes, and review of procurement documentation.

[32]These visits took place in Waleska, Georgia; Ball, Louisiana; Saugus, Massachusetts; Newark, Ohio; Parma, Ohio; and Bremerton, Washington.

[33]EPA Office of Inspector General, *American Recovery and Reinvestment Act Site Inspection of the Clean Water State Revolving Fund Projects at the City of Long Beach, California,* 11-R-0082 (Feb. 1, 2011).

[34]EPA Office of Inspector General, *American Recovery and Reinvestment Act Site Visit of the Denver Street Storage Project, City of Astoria, Oregon,* 11-R-0172 (Mar. 22, 2011).

funds for all programs—had resulted.[35] As the EPA Inspector General noted in May 2011, however, fraud schemes can take time to surface. The Inspector General cited an ongoing investigation of a foreign company that received over $1.1 million in contracts for equipment to be used in wastewater treatment facilities across the United States after falsely certifying that the equipment met the Recovery Act Buy American provision.[36] Furthermore, the Inspector General also testified that EPA Region 6 officials identified, through a hotline tip, $1 million in unallowable grant costs charged by seven subrecipients. These funds have been reprogrammed by the state for other uses.[37]

State Officials Said They Have Found Few Problems during Site Visits to Monitor Recovery Act Projects

EPA's oversight plan indicates that state officials should visit each project site at least once per year, and suggests that state officials review the items on EPA's state Recovery Act inspection checklist, or a similar state-specific checklist. According to the plan, state officials should complete the checklist and inform regional offices of any issues encountered in the oversight reviews, inspections, or audits.

According to program officials in the nine states we reviewed, the clean and drinking water SRF projects they reviewed largely complied with Recovery Act requirements. The officials said that they inspected each Recovery Act project site at least once during the course of project construction, and sometimes more frequently, depending on the complexity of the project. These officials also said that, using the EPA or other checklist, they evaluated whether the communities or subrecipients were meeting Recovery Act reporting requirements. For example, according to the checklist, officials verified whether subrecipients submitted FTE information to the state each quarter, and whether they submitted regular reports certifying that the project remained in compliance with the Davis-Bacon provisions, based on a weekly review of payroll records. In addition, the officials used the checklist to review the

---

[35]The Honorable Earl E. Devaney, Chairman, Recovery Accountability and Transparency Board, Testimony before the Committee on Oversight and Government Reform, U.S. House of Representatives, June 14, 2011.

[36]EPA Office of Inspector General, *Stimulus Status: Two Years and Counting*, Statement of Arthur A. Elkins, Jr. Inspector General, Before the Committee on Transportation and Infrastructure, U.S. House of Representatives, May 4, 2011.

[37]EPA Office of Inspector General, *Stimulus Status: Two Years and Counting*, Statement of Arthur A. Elkins, Jr. Inspector General, Before the Committee on Transportation and Infrastructure, U.S. House of Representatives, May 4, 2011.

contents of project files and ensure that key project documents were present, such as project-specific waivers. Using the checklist, these officials also confirmed that projects receiving green infrastructure funding properly incorporated green components. In addition, officials in Alabama, Connecticut, Nevada, and New Mexico took photographs of various project components to record compliance with the Buy American provisions.

A few officials in the nine states that we reviewed said that meeting the oversight plan requirements, such as increasing the number of site visits, has been time-consuming. However, a couple of officials said that their site visits have resulted in better subrecipient compliance with Recovery Act requirements. For example, as a result of their site visits, state officials corrected a problem they had identified—subrecipients in three of the nine states we reviewed had foreign components on site:

- In New Mexico, officials told us that foreign components had been shipped to a project site, and that they had to replace the components before incorporating them into the project.

- Missouri officials said that the EPA inspection checklist had helped to identify some foreign-made components on a project site, and the components were replaced.

- Connecticut officials told us that they had identified a drinking water project that contained Chinese and German equipment valued at $10,000. They said that the project was already in service, making replacement costly and impractical because it would require consumers to be without water. The state is working with EPA to resolve the matter.

State Audit Reports Covering Clean and Drinking Water Programs Found Few Significant Problems

State auditors—or private auditors contracted by the states—helped ensure the appropriate use of Recovery Act water funds. For eight of the nine states that we reviewed, we received state or private audits that examined the Recovery Act Clean and Drinking Water SRF programs. With the following two exceptions, the auditors have reported few significant problems:[38]

- *Michigan.* In its audit of the Michigan Department of Environmental Quality's fiscal year 2008 and 2009 financial statements, the Michigan Office of the Auditor General reported several material weaknesses in internal controls and material noncompliance with requirements related to subrecipient monitoring and other special provisions for Recovery Act-funded expenditures. For example, for the Recovery Act Clean and Drinking Water SRF programs, the auditors found that the Michigan Department of Environmental Quality overstated the number of FTEs for the reporting period ending September 30, 2009, because its methodology for calculating FTEs was not in accordance with June 2009 OMB guidance. The auditors also found that the department did not have a process to (1) verify the accuracy of the information contained in its recipient report; (2) adequately monitor subrecipients' expending of Recovery Act funds for construction activities to ensure that the subrecipients complied with the Davis-Bacon provisions; and (3) adequately monitor subrecipients' expending of Recovery Act funds for the construction, alteration, maintenance, or repair of a public building or public work to ensure that the subrecipients complied with Buy American provisions. In response to these findings, the auditors recommended that the department improve its internal control over the SRF programs to ensure compliance with federal laws and regulations. The department partially or wholly agreed with these findings, and anticipated taking the appropriate corrective action by September 30, 2011.[39] One Michigan official said that corrective action has been implemented for the findings that pertain to the SRF program.

- *Washington State.* In the November 2010 Financial Statements and Federal Compliance report for the Drinking Water SRF program,

---

[38]According to one official, Nevada has not conducted an audit on the Recovery Act Clean and Drinking Water SRF program and is considering auditing the program in fiscal year 2011. Auditors in Alabama, Connecticut, Maryland, Missouri, New Mexico, and Wyoming reported no significant problems.

[39]Michigan Office of the Auditor General, *Financial Audit Including the Provisions of the Single Audit Act of the Department of Environmental Quality, October 1, 2007 through September 30, 2009*, No. 761-0100-10, (June 2010).

auditors found significant deficiencies in the Department of Health's internal control.[40] As a result, they recommended that the Department of Health train employees on financial reporting preparation and requirements; establish and follow internal controls, including an appropriate, independent review of the financial statements and related schedules; and establish policies and procedures related to the preparation of the year-end financial statements. The Department of Health concurred with the finding, and stated that it would take appropriate action. In the corresponding report for the Clean Water SRF program, auditors found no internal control weaknesses.

Federal and State Agencies Continue to Oversee the Quality of Recipient Reporting Data, Including Jobs, in Seventh Round of Reporting

To meet our mandate to comment on recipient reports, we have continued monitoring recipient-reported data, including data on jobs funded. For this report, we focused our review on SRF program funds and EPA and state efforts to conduct data quality reviews and identify and remediate reporting problems.

EPA Continued Performing Data Quality Checks and Said Data Quality Is Relatively Stable

According to EPA officials, the overall quality of the states' SRF data on Recovery.gov, which EPA officials have checked each quarter, is stable. The officials said that the states' initial unfamiliarity with a newly developed reporting system has been resolved, the Federalreporting.gov help desk has improved, and guidance issued by OMB has clarified reporting issues over time. During the seventh round of reporting, which ended on March 31, 2011, EPA officials continued to perform data quality checks as they had in previous quarters. Specifically, EPA used data from the agency's grants database, contracts database, and financial management system to compare with recipient-reported data. These systems contain authoritative data for every award made to the states, including the award identification number, award date, award amount, outlays, Treasury Account Symbol codes, and recipient names. According

---

[40]Washington State Auditor's Office, *Financial Statements and Federal Compliance Report, Department of Health Drinking Water State Revolving Fund, July 1, 2008 through July 30, 2009*, No. 1004482 (November 1, 2010).

to EPA officials, they use the agency data to ensure that recipient-reported information for a given award corresponds with the information on EPA's official award documents. EPA staff can raise questions about any inconsistent data through the Federalreporting.gov system. State recipients may make appropriate changes to the data through the end of the reporting period, and after public release, during the continuous correction cycle. According to EPA officials, this process has resolved any questions and comments from EPA's reviews.

To facilitate its oversight of state-reported data, EPA required states to use its Clean Water Benefits Reporting (CBR) system and Program Benefits Reporting (PBR) system to report on certain Recovery Act project information, such as the project name, contract date, construction start, Recovery Act funding, jobs created or retained, and project purpose and anticipated benefits.[41] EPA officials said that they do not routinely collect state expenditure data in these systems and that they rely on regional officials to review expenditures reported by the states on Recovery.gov. We compared EPA's data on awards and funds drawn down by states with data reported by states on Recovery.gov and found only a few minor inconsistencies in the data.

Similarly, in September 2010, EPA's OIG reported that the Recovery.gov data for EPA's SRF programs contained a low rate of errors.[42] The OIG audited EPA's controls for reviewing recipient-reported data after the second round of reporting, which ended December 31, 2009, comparing EPA data on award type, award number, funding agency code, award agency code, and award amount to state-reported data on Recovery.gov. The OIG report found that EPA's controls helped lower the rate of errors for these key data and recommended some improvements to EPA's process. EPA's Clean and Drinking Water SRF program officials said that they have had few errors in the SRF data in the last three rounds of reporting.

---

[41]The CBR system was an existing system the states used to report information on clean water SRF projects, while the PBR system was a new system being tested to allow states to report drinking water SRF project information.

[42]EPA Office of Inspector General, *EPA Effectively Reviewed Recovery Act Recipient Data but Opportunities for Improvement Exist* (Washington, D.C., Sept. 27, 2010).

Nine States Checked Quality of Recovery Act Data Quarterly, but Minor FTE Discrepancies Occurred

Officials in the nine states we reviewed indicated that the quality of recipient data has remained relatively stable, although we found that the states differed in how they reported state agencies' FTE data and did not report some subrecipients' FTE data. Water program officials in these states said that they check the quality of data that are reported on Federalreporting.gov and then Recovery.gov. In addition, officials in Alabama, Connecticut, Maryland, Missouri, and New Mexico said that they examined payroll data submitted by contractors to verify FTE data. In some cases, state officials said that they contact subrecipients for clarification about data that are missing or inconsistent.

In addition to department-level checks, in most of the nine states we reviewed, state-level Recovery Office staff checked the data before submitting the information to Federalreporting.gov. In four of the nine states—Alabama, Maryland, Missouri, and New Mexico—Recovery Office staff monitored Recovery Act implementation and performed independent data quality checks of the data reported by state agencies. According to several state officials, this reporting structure provided an additional level of review of state agency data. In Maryland, for example, officials said that their state-level reporting system relieves subrecipients of certain reporting duties. Subrecipients submitted the FTE and payroll information to Maryland's StateStat office, and staff in that office reviewed and validated the data, completed the required federal reports, and submitted them to Federalreporting.gov. Furthermore, for control purposes, only two staff members handled the information. In addition, staff in Nevada's Recovery Office conducted quality checks; however, each state agency then submitted its data directly to the appropriate federal agency. The remaining four states—Connecticut, Michigan, Washington State, and Wyoming—did not have a Recovery Office staff check data quality.

We found minor problems with the FTE data that some of the nine states reported. Specifically, (1) states differed in how they reported the FTEs associated with their own program staff—that is, those who conduct document reviews, site inspections, and other key program duties; and (2) three states identified missing or incorrectly reported FTE data on Recovery.gov, and these data have not been corrected. In particular:

- Six of the nine states reported the FTEs for their state employees who were paid with Recovery Act funds, while two states did not.[43] Officials

---

[43]One state did not take Recovery Act funds to pay for its state employees' time on Recovery Act work.

in Maryland and Michigan noted that they did not report all the time their state employees spent on program activities in Federalreporting.gov, although these FTEs were paid for with Recovery Act funds. EPA officials said that they provided states with OMB guidance and that OMB guidance requires states to report FTEs paid for with Recovery Act funds.

- Washington State officials who administer the Clean Water SRF program changed the time frame for reporting FTE data in the third round of reporting, and as a result, missed reporting one quarter of data. During the first two reporting rounds, because some subrecipients were finding it difficult to submit complete FTE data to the state by the state's deadline, staff reported data from 2 months of the current quarter and 1 month of the previous quarter. During the third reporting quarter, the state began reporting 3 months of current data. However, the state received data from a subrecipient after the deadline for reporting and did not correct the data during the correction period. As a result, officials said about 18 FTEs remain unreported. EPA officials told them to keep a record of these FTEs in case there is an opportunity to correct the data.

- Officials in New Mexico did not report a few FTEs for the state's Drinking Water SRF program in the first two rounds of reporting. The officials explained that the revisions were submitted to the state after the reporting period ended and therefore the FTEs were not captured in Recovery.gov.

- Officials in Wyoming identified incorrectly reported FTEs for two quarters. The FTEs were incorrect because the state entered the data for one clean water project for one quarter in the next quarter. As a result, one quarter's data were overstated by a few FTEs, and the other quarter's data were understated by a few FTEs. The state official explained that the data changed after they were initially reported in Recovery.gov and were not updated during the correction period.

As the bulk of Recovery Act funding is spent, EPA officials said that the states were beginning to complete their projects. Officials said that before the next reporting round begins in July 2011, they plan to issue a memorandum to states on how to complete their Recovery Act grants and when to stop reporting to Recovery.gov. During the seventh round of reporting, one state in each program indicated in Recovery.gov that the grant—including all projects that received money from the grant—was complete. EPA officials told us that as of early May 2011, 629 clean water and 383 drinking water projects have been completed across all states.

Some state officials charged with coordinating state-level Recovery Act funds also said that they are winding down their activities. In Michigan, for example, the Recovery Office was originally a separate office under the Governor, but has since been moved under the Department of Management and Budget. In Nevada, the Recovery Act Director said that his office will be eliminated at the end of June 2011. At that point, the Department of Administration's centralized grant office will take responsibility for Nevada's remaining Recovery Act efforts. Similarly, officials at the New Mexico Office of Recovery and Reinvestment said that their office is currently funded through the Recovery Act State Fiscal Stabilization Fund through the end of June 2011.

Because of the high-level nature of SRF recipient reporting for Recovery.gov and the availability of information in its own data systems, EPA officials do not anticipate using data from Recovery.gov. The officials said that whereas Recovery.gov summarizes information on many projects at the state level, the data from CBR and PBR are more useful for understanding states' projects than data on Recovery.gov because the internal data are provided by project and include more detail. EPA officials said that by the end of 2011 they plan to use information in these two internal systems to assess anticipated benefits of the Recovery Act SRF program funds. EPA Clean Water officials said that they would perform case studies of completed projects and assess anticipated benefits. Drinking Water officials said that they are considering three major studies, some joint with the Clean Water SRF program. These studies may include assessments of project distributions, green projects' benefits, and subsidy beneficiaries.

The States Identified Challenges in Implementing Recovery Act SRF Programs That Highlight Potential Future Challenges for SRF Programs

Our May 2010 report identified the challenge of maintaining accountability for Recovery Act funds and recommended improved monitoring of Recovery Act funds by EPA and the states.[44] As we note above, our current work shows that EPA and the nine states we reviewed have made progress in addressing this challenge. Two challenges EPA and state officials identified in spending Recovery Act SRF program funds may continue as requirements introduced with the Recovery Act are incorporated into the base SRF programs. Specifically, in fiscal years 2010 and 2011, the Clean and Drinking Water SRF programs were required to include provisions for green projects and additional subsidies.

Encouraging green projects. The effort to support green projects was included in EPA's fiscal year 2010 and 2011 appropriations for the base Clean and Drinking Water SRF programs. As we discussed above, under the requirement to fund green projects in the Recovery Act, in certain cases state officials said they had to choose between a green water project and a project that was otherwise ranked higher to address water quality problems. Similarly, in our May 2010 report, we found that officials in some of the states we reviewed said that they gave preference to green projects for funding purposes, and sometimes ranked those projects above another project with higher public health benefits. In addition to competing priorities for funding, EPA's OIG found, in its February 2010 report, that a lack of clear guidance on the "green requirement" caused confusion and disagreements as to which projects were eligible for green funding.[45] Officials in two of the nine states we reviewed noted that the goal of supporting green projects was not difficult to achieve because they had already identified green projects. Officials in four other states said that while they all met the 20 percent green project goal, it was difficult to achieve, leading one official to suggest that green projects be encouraged without setting a fixed percentage of program funds. EPA officials added that they had also heard that achieving the green requirement may continue to be difficult in some states, particularly for the Drinking Water program. However, the officials also said that they were encouraging states to include green components in their drinking water projects rather than seeking solely green projects.

---

[44]GAO-10-604.

[45]EPA Office of Inspector General, *Evaluation Report: EPA Needs Definitive Guidance for Recovery Act and Future Green Reserve Projects*, Report No. 10-R-0057 (Washington, D.C., Feb. 1, 2010).

Providing additional subsidies. The fiscal years 2010 and 2011 appropriations for the Clean and Drinking Water SRF programs also continued the requirement to provide additional subsidies in the form of principal forgiveness, negative interest loans, or grants. The subsidy provisions reduced the funds available to use as a subsidy from a minimum of 50 percent of funds required under the Recovery Act to a minimum of 30 percent of base SRF program funds.[46] As with the Recovery Act, the appropriations in fiscal years 2010 and 2011 do not require this additional subsidy to be targeted to any types of projects or communities with economic need,[47] and as the recent EPA OIG report notes, there are no requirements for EPA or the states to track how these subsidies are used. The base Clean and Drinking Water SRF programs were created to be a sustainable source of funding for communities' water and wastewater infrastructure through the continued repayment of loans to states. Officials in four of the nine states we reviewed identified a potential challenge in continuing to provide a specific amount of subsidies while sustaining the Clean and Drinking Water SRF programs as revolving funds. State officials pointed out that when monies are not repaid into the revolving fund, the reuse of funds is reduced and the purpose of the revolving SRF program changes from primarily providing loans for investments in water infrastructure to providing grants.

Agency Comments and Our Evaluation

We provided a draft of the report to the Environmental Protection Agency for review and comment. EPA stated that it did not have any comments on our report.

We are sending copies of this report to the appropriate congressional committees, Administrator of the Environmental Protection Agency, and other interested parties. In addition, this report is available at no charge on the GAO Web site at http://www.gao.gov.

---

[46]For the Clean Water SRF program, the 30 percent minimum only applies to the portion of appropriated funds exceeding $1 billion.

[47]The Drinking Water SRF program had a subsidy provision that allowed states to use up to 30 percent of their annual grant to provide additional subsidies to help economically disadvantaged communities. 42 U.S.C. § 300j-12(d).

If you or your staff members have any questions about this report, please contact me at (202) 512-3841 or trimbled@gao.gov. Contact points for our Offices of Congressional Relations and Public Affairs may be found on the last page of this report. GAO staff who made major contributions to this report are listed in appendix III.

David C. Trimble
Acting Director
Natural Resources and Environment

The Honorable Daniel K. Inouye
Chairman
The Honorable Thad Cochran
Vice Chairman
Committee on Appropriations
United States Senate

The Honorable Harold Rogers
Chairman
The Honorable Norman D. Dicks
Ranking Member
Committee on Appropriations
House of Representatives

The Honorable Joseph I. Lieberman
Chairman
The Honorable Susan M. Collins
Ranking Member
Committee on Homeland Security
    and Governmental Affairs
United States Senate

The Honorable Darrell E. Issa
Chairman
The Honorable Elijah Cummings
Ranking Member
Committee on Oversight
    and Government Reform
House of Representatives

The Honorable Barbara Boxer
Chairwoman
The Honorable James M. Inhofe
Ranking Member
Committee on Environment
    and Public Works
United States Senate

The Honorable Fred Upton
Chairman
The Honorable Henry Waxman
Ranking Member
Committee on Energy and Commerce
House of Representatives

The Honorable John L. Mica
Chairman
The Honorable Nick J. Rahall
Ranking Member
Committee on Transportation
    and Infrastructure
House of Representatives

Appendix I: Objectives, Scope, and Methodology

The objectives of this review were to examine the (1) status and use of American Recovery and Reinvestment Act of 2009 (Recovery Act) Clean and Drinking Water State Revolving Funds (SRF) program funds nationwide and in selected states; (2) actions taken by federal, state, and other agencies to monitor and ensure accountability of these program funds; (3) approaches federal agencies and selected states have taken to ensure data quality, including data for jobs reported by recipients of these program funds; and (4) challenges, if any, that states have faced in implementing Recovery Act requirements for the Clean and Drinking Water SRF programs.

To examine the status and use of Recovery Act funds nationwide and in selected states, we reviewed relevant Clean and Drinking Water SRF federal laws, regulations, and guidance, and examined federal and selected state program and project documentation. We interviewed Environmental Protection Agency (EPA) officials responsible for administering programs in headquarters. We also interviewed state Recovery Act officials and state program officials, in environmental and public health departments, who are responsible for revolving loan fund programs.

We obtained and analyzed nationwide Recovery Act data from the EPA Clean Water SRF Benefits Reporting (CBR) system and the Drinking Water SRF Project Benefits Reporting (PBR) system for all states. These data included (1) categories of clean and drinking water infrastructure and green projects; (2) Recovery Act funds awarded and drawn down from the Treasury; (3) amount of subsidization (principal forgiveness or grants and low- or no-interest loans); and (4) number of full-time equivalents (FTE). We also obtained and analyzed key nationwide data from the EPA National Information Management System on Recovery Act funding by type of clean water project. Using these data, we summarized the amount of Recovery Act funds provided by states to clean and drinking water SRF projects by category of project (e.g., clean water sanitary sewer overflow and drinking water treatment). We assessed these data for their reliability and determined that they were reliable for our purposes.

To develop a more in-depth view of the states' use of Recovery Act funds for Clean and Drinking Water SRF programs, we selected a nonprobability sample of nine states we had not reviewed in our previous bimonthly

reports, representing all but 1 of the 10 EPA regions.[1] The states we
selected were Alabama, Connecticut, Maryland, Michigan, Missouri, New
Mexico, Nevada, Washington State, and Wyoming. For each state, we
interviewed officials from the state environmental department or public
health program (water program officials) to discuss their use of Recovery
Act SRF program funds. We conducted these interviews using a data
collection instrument to obtain consistent information from the states on
their water problems and ranking systems for prioritizing projects for
funding; the amount of funds provided to projects; the allocation of
funding and subsidization to green projects, small communities, and
economically disadvantaged communities; the amount of funds received
and spent, and the number of FTE positions funded for each project and in
total. Additionally, in Alabama, Maryland, and New Mexico, we visited a
total of five clean and drinking water projects funded with Recovery Act
funds.

To examine the actions that federal, state, and other agencies have taken
to monitor and ensure accountability for Recovery Act SRF program
funds, we reviewed and analyzed relevant federal guidance and
documentation, including EPA's oversight plan for Recovery Act projects.
To determine whether EPA was following its oversight plan, we reviewed
at least one EPA Recovery Act program evaluation report for the Clean
Water and Drinking Water programs for all 50 states for fiscal years 2009
or 2010. We also reviewed EPA headquarters' reviews of regional reports
that detailed the performance of regional drinking water staff as they
monitored and documented the states' implementation of the Drinking
Water SRF program, and we asked headquarters staff about the reviews of
regional clean water staff that they conducted, but did not document. To
develop a more in-depth view of the states' monitoring processes, we
asked program officials in the nine states to respond to questions about
their oversight activities in our data collection instrument. We then
interviewed state program officials who were responsible for monitoring
and oversight about their oversight activities and efforts to ensure that
projects complied with Recovery Act requirements, including their
processes for inspecting project sites and their procedures for collecting
and reporting Recovery Act SRF program data. In addition, we interviewed
Recovery Act officials in the six states that had such staff—Alabama,

---

[1]We did not select any states in EPA Region 2—which includes New Jersey, New York, and
Puerto Rico—because we had reviewed New Jersey and New York in previous Recovery
Act reports.

Maryland, Missouri, Nevada, New Mexico, and Washington—about their
oversight of program staff, data quality, and federal reporting during
additional interviews. Furthermore, to develop an understanding of the
work that the broader audit community has completed on the Recovery
Act Clean and Drinking Water SRF programs, we reviewed all relevant
EPA Office of Inspector General reports that were published since we
issued our previous report on the Recovery Act SRF programs in May
2010.[2]

To examine approaches federal agencies and selected states have taken to
ensure data quality for jobs reported by Recovery Act recipients, we
conducted work at both the national and state level. The recipient
reporting section of this report responds to the Recovery Act's mandate
that we comment on the estimates of jobs created or retained by direct
recipients of Recovery Act funds. For our national review of the seventh
submission of recipient reports, covering the period from January 1, 2011,
through March 31, 2011, we continued our monitoring of errors or
potential problems by repeating many of the analyses and edit checks
reported in our six prior reviews covering the period from February 2009
through December 31, 2010.[3] To examine how the quality of jobs data
reported by recipients of Clean and Drinking Water SRF grants has
changed over time, we compared the seven quarters of recipient reporting
data that were publicly available at Recovery.gov on April 30, 2011. We
performed edit checks and other analyses on the Clean and Drinking
Water SRF prime recipient reports and compared funding data from EPA
with funding amounts reported on the recipient reports. We also reviewed
documentation and interviewed federal agency officials from EPA who are
responsible for ensuring a reasonable degree of quality across their
programs' recipient reports.

At the state level, we interviewed state officials in the nine states we
reviewed about the policies and procedures they had in place to ensure
that FTE information for Recovery Act projects was reported accurately.
For selected Recovery Act data fields, we asked state program officials in

---

[2]GAO-10-604.

[3]As we did with the prior reviews, we conducted these checks and analyses on all prime
recipient reports to assess data logic and consistency and identify unusual or atypical data.
For this seventh review, we continued to see similar results with minor variations in the
number or percent of reports appearing atypical or showing some form of data
discrepancy.

the nine states to review and verify EPA's Recovery Act data from CBR
and PBR and provide corrected data where applicable. For the nine states,
we compared state-reported Clean and Drinking Water SRF FTE data from
the sixth submission of recipient reports, the period covering October 1,
2010, through December 31, 2010, with corresponding data reported on
Recovery.gov. We addressed any discrepancies between these two sets of
data by contacting state program officials. Our national and state work in
selected states showed agreement between EPA recipient information and
the information reported by recipients directly to Federalreporting.gov. In
general, we consider the data used to be sufficiently reliable for purposes
of this report. The results of our FTE analyses are limited to the two SRF
water programs and time periods reviewed and are not generalizable to
any other program's FTE reporting.

To examine challenges that states have faced in implementing Recovery
Act requirements, we interviewed state SRF program officials using a data
collection instrument and obtained information on challenges state
program officials told us pertaining to the 20 percent green project
requirement and the subsidization requirement.

We conducted this performance audit from September 2010 through June
2011 in accordance with generally accepted government auditing
standards. Those standards require that we plan and perform the audit to
obtain sufficient, appropriate evidence to provide a reasonable basis for
our findings and conclusions based on our audit objectives. We believe
that the evidence obtained provides a reasonable basis for our findings
and conclusions based on our audit objectives.

Appendix II: Status of Prior Open Recommendations and Matters for Congressional Consideration

In this appendix, we update the status of agencies' efforts to implement the 26 open recommendations, and 2 newly implemented recommendations from our previous bimonthly and recipient reporting reviews.[1] Recommendations that were listed as implemented or closed in a prior report are not repeated here. Lastly, we address the status of our Matters for Congressional Consideration.

Department of Energy

Open Recommendations[2]

Given the concerns we have raised about whether program requirements were being met, we recommended in May 2010 that the Department of Energy (DOE), in conjunction with both state and local weatherization agencies, develop and clarify weatherization program guidance that

- clarifies the specific methodology for calculating the average cost per home weatherized to ensure that the maximum average cost limit is applied as intended.

- accelerates current DOE efforts to develop national standards for weatherization training, certification, and accreditation, which is currently expected to take 2 years to complete.

---

[1]GAO, *Recovery Act: As Initial Implementation Unfolds in States and Localities, Continued Attention to Accountability Issues Is Essential*, GAO-09-580 (Washington, D.C.: Apr. 23, 2009); *Recovery Act: States' and Localities' Current and Planned Uses of Funds While Facing Fiscal Stresses*, GAO-09-829 (Washington, D.C.: July 8, 2009); *Recovery Act: Funds Continue to Provide Fiscal Relief to States and Localities, While Accountability and Reporting Challenges Need to Be Fully Addressed*, GAO-09-1016 (Washington, D.C.: Sept. 23, 2009); *Recovery Act: Recipient Reported Jobs Data Provide Some Insight into Use of Recovery Act Funding, but Data Quality and Reporting Issues Need Attention*, GAO-10-223 (Washington, D.C.: Nov. 19, 2009); *Recovery Act: Status of States' and Localities' Use of Funds and Efforts to Ensure Accountability*, GAO-10-231 (Washington, D.C.: Dec. 10, 2009); *Recovery Act: One Year Later, States' and Localities' Uses of Funds and Opportunities to Strengthen Accountability*, GAO-10-437 (Washington, D.C.: Mar. 3, 2010); *Recovery Act: States' and Localities' Uses of Funds and Actions Needed to Address Implementation Challenges and Bolster Accountability*, GAO-10-604 (Washington, D.C.: May 26, 2010); *Recovery Act: Opportunities to Improve Management and Strengthen Accountability over States' and Localities' Uses of Funds*, GAO-10-999 (Washington, D.C.: Sept. 20, 2010); *Recovery Act: Head Start Grantees Expand Services, but More Consistent Communication Could Improve Accountability and Decisions about Spending*, GAO-11-166 (Washington, D.C.: Dec. 15, 2010); and *Recovery Act: Energy Efficiency and Conservation Block Grant Recipients Face Challenges Meeting Legislative and Program Goals and Requirements*, GAO-11-379 (Washington, D.C.: Apr. 7, 2011).

[2]GAO-11-379, 48-50.

- develops a best practice guide for key internal controls that should be present at the local weatherization agency level to ensure compliance with key program requirements.

- sets time frames for development and implementation of state monitoring programs.

- revisits the various methodologies used in determining the weatherization work that should be performed based on the consideration of cost-effectiveness and develops standard methodologies that ensure that priority is given to the most cost-effective weatherization work. To validate any methodologies created, this effort should include the development of standards for accurately measuring the long-term energy savings resulting from weatherization work conducted.

In addition, given that state and local agencies have felt pressure to meet a large increase in production targets while effectively meeting program requirements and have experienced some confusion over production targets, funding obligations, and associated consequences for not meeting production and funding goals, we recommended that DOE clarify its production targets, funding deadlines, and associated consequences while providing a balanced emphasis on the importance of meeting program requirements.

Agency Actions

DOE generally concurred with these recommendations and has made some progress on implementing them. For example, to clarify the methodology for calculating the average cost per home, DOE has developed draft guidance to help grantees develop consistency in their average cost per unit calculations. The guidance further clarifies the general cost categories that are included in the average cost per home. DOE anticipates issuance of the guidance in June 2011.

DOE has also taken steps to address our recommendation that it develop and clarify guidance to generate a best practice guide for key internal controls. DOE distributed a memorandum dated May 13, 2011 to grantees reminding them of their responsibilities to ensure compliance with internal controls and the consequences of failing to do so. This memo is currently under internal review and DOE anticipates it will be released in May 2011.

Open Recommendations[3]

To better ensure that Energy Efficiency and Conservation Block Grant (EECBG) funds are used to meet Recovery Act and program goals, we recommended in April 2011 that DOE, take the following actions:

- Explore a means to capture information on the monitoring processes of all recipients to make certain that recipients have effective monitoring practices.

- Solicit information from recipients regarding the methodology they used to calculate their energy-related impact metrics and verify that recipients who use DOE's estimation tool use the most recent version when calculating these metrics.

Agency Actions

DOE generally concurred with these recommendations, stating that "implementing the report's recommendations will help ensure that the Program continues to be well managed and executed." DOE also provided additional information on steps it has initiated or planned to implement. In particular, with respect to our first recommendation, DOE elaborated on additional monitoring practices it performs over high dollar value grant recipients, such as its reliance on audit results obtained in accordance with the Single Audit Act and its update to the EECBG program requirements in the Compliance Supplement to OMB Circular No. A-133. However, these monitoring practices only focus on larger grant recipients, and we believe that the program could be more effectively monitored if DOE captured information on the monitoring practices of all recipients. With respect to our second recommendation, DOE officials said that in order to provide a reasonable estimate of energy savings, the program currently reviews energy process and impact metrics submitted each quarter for reasonableness, works with grantees to correct unreasonable metrics, and works with grantees through closeout to refine metrics. In addition, DOE officials said that they plan to take a scientific approach to overall program evaluation during the formal evaluation process at the conclusion of the program, which will occur in December 2012. However, DOE has not yet identified any specific plans to solicit information from recipients regarding the methodology they used to calculate their energy-related impact metrics or to verify that recipients who use DOE's estimation tool use the most recent version when calculating.

---

[3]GAO-11-379, 36-47.

Environmental Protection Agency

Newly Implemented
Recommendation[4]

We recommended that the Environmental Protection Agency (EPA) Administrator work with the states to implement specific oversight procedures to monitor and ensure subrecipients' compliance with the provisions of the Recovery Act-funded Clean Water and Drinking Water State Revolving Fund (SRF) program.

Agency Actions

In part in response to our recommendation, EPA provided additional guidance to the states regarding their oversight responsibilities, with an emphasis on enhancing site-specific inspections. Specifically, in June 2010, the agency developed and issued an oversight plan outline for Recovery Act projects that provides guidance on the frequency, content, and documentation related to regional reviews of state Recovery Act programs and regional and state reviews of specific Recovery Act projects. We found that EPA regions have reviewed all 50 states' Clean and Drinking Water SRF programs at least once since the Recovery Act was enacted, and have generally carried out the oversight instructions in EPA's plan. For example, regional officials reviewed files with state documents and information to ensure proper controls over Davis-Bacon, Buy American, and other Recovery Act requirements. Regional staff also visited one drinking water project in every state, but did not meet this goal for clean water projects due to time and budget constraints. We also found that EPA headquarters officials have been reviewing the regions' performance evaluation reports for states, and the officials said that they implemented a 60-day time frame for completing these reports. In the nine states that we reviewed in this report, program officials described their site visits to projects and the use of the EPA inspection checklist (or state equivalent), according to EPA's oversight plan. State officials told us that they visit their Recovery Act projects at least once during construction and sometimes more frequently depending on the complexity of the project. We consider these agency actions to have addressed our recommendation.

---

[4]GAO-10-604, 246-247.

Department of Health and Human Services: Office of Head Start

Open Recommendation[5]

To oversee the extent to which grantees are meeting the program goal of providing services to children and families and to better track the initiation of services under the Recovery Act, we recommended that the Director of the Office of Head Start (OHS) should collect data on the extent to which children and pregnant women actually receive services from Head Start and Early Head Start grantees.

Agency Actions

The Department of Health and Human Services (HHS) disagreed with our recommendation. OHS officials stated that attendance data are adequately examined in triennial or yearly on-site reviews and in periodic risk management meetings. Because these reviews and meetings do not collect or report data on service provision, we continue to believe that tracking services to children and families is an important measure of the work undertaken by Head Start and Early Head Start service providers.

Open Recommendation[6]

To help ensure that grantees report consistent enrollment figures, we recommended that the Director of OHS should better communicate a consistent definition of "enrollment" to grantees for monthly and yearly reporting and begin verifying grantees' definition of "enrollment" during triennial reviews.

Agency Actions

OHS issued informal guidance on its Web site clarifying monthly reporting requirements to make them consistent with annual enrollment reporting. While this guidance directs grantees to include in enrollment counts all children and pregnant mothers who have received a specified minimum of services, it could be further clarified by specifying that counts should include only those children and pregnant mothers. According to HHS officials, OHS is considering further regulatory clarification.

---

[5]GAO-10-604, 184.

[6]GAO-11-166, 39.

Open Recommendation[7]	To provide grantees consistent information on how and when they will be expected to obligate and expend federal funds, we recommended that the Director of OHS should clearly communicate its policy to grantees for carrying over or extending the use of Recovery Act funds from one fiscal year into the next.

Agency Actions

HHS indicated that OHS will issue guidance to grantees on obligation and expenditure requirements, as well as improve efforts to effectively communicate the mechanisms in place for grantees to meet the requirements for obligation and expenditure of funds.

Open Recommendation[8]	To better consider known risks in scoping and staffing required reviews of Recovery Act grantees, we recommended that the Director of OHS should direct OHS regional offices to consistently perform and document Risk Management Meetings and incorporate known risks, including financial management risks, into the process for staffing and conducting reviews.

Agency Actions

HHS reported that OHS is reviewing the risk management process to ensure it is consistently performed and documented in its centralized data system and that it has taken related steps, such as requiring the Grant Officer to identify known or suspected risks prior to an on-site review.

Newly Implemented Recommendation[9]	To facilitate understanding of whether regional decisions regarding waivers of the program's matching requirement are consistent with Recovery Act grantees' needs across regions, we recommended that the Director of OHS should regularly review waivers of the nonfederal matching requirement and associated justifications.

Agency Actions

HHS reports that it has taken actions to address our recommendation. For example, HHS reports that OHS has conducted a review of waivers of the

---

[7]GAO-11-166, 39.

[8]GAO-11-166, 39.

[9]GAO-10-604, 184.

nonfederal matching requirement and tracked all waivers in the Web-based data system. HHS further reports that OHS has determined that they are reasonably consistent across regions.

Department of Housing and Urban Development

Open Recommendation[10]

Because the absence of third-party investors reduces the amount of overall scrutiny Tax Credit Assistance Program (TCAP) projects would receive and the Department of Housing and Urban Development (HUD) is currently not aware of how many projects lacked third-party investors, we recommended that HUD should develop a risk-based plan for its role in overseeing TCAP projects that recognizes the level of oversight provided by others.

Agency Actions

HUD responded to our recommendation by saying it will identify projects that are not funded by the HOME Investment Partnerships Program (HOME) funds and projects that have a nominal tax credit award. However, HUD said it will not be able to identify these projects until it could access the data needed to perform the analysis, and it does not receive access to those data until after projects have been completed. HUD currently has not taken any action on this recommendation because it only has data on the small percentage of projects completed to date. It is too early in the process to be able to identify projects that lack third-party investors. The agency will take action once they are able to collect the necessary information from the project owners and the state housing finance agencies.

[10]GAO-10-999, 189.

Department of Labor

Open Recommendations[11]

To enhance the Department of Labor's (Labor) ability to manage its Recovery Act and regular Workforce Investment Act (WIA) formula grants and to build on its efforts to improve the accuracy and consistency of financial reporting, we recommended that the Secretary of Labor take the following actions:

- To determine the extent and nature of reporting inconsistencies across the states and better target technical assistance, conduct a one-time assessment of financial reports that examines whether each state's reported data on obligations meet Labor's requirements.

- To enhance state accountability and to facilitate their progress in making reporting improvements, routinely review states' reporting on obligations during regular state comprehensive reviews.

Agency Actions

Labor agreed with both of our recommendations and has begun to take some actions to implement them. To determine the extent of reporting inconsistencies, Labor awarded a contract in September 2010 to perform an assessment of state financial reports to determine if the data reported are accurate and reflect Labor's guidance on reporting of obligations and expenditures. Since then, Labor has completed interviews with all states and is preparing a report of the findings. To enhance states' accountability and facilitate their progress in making improvements in reporting, Labor has drafted guidance on the definitions of key financial terms such as "obligations," which is currently in final clearance. After the guidance is issued, Labor plans to conduct a systemwide webinar and interactive training on this topic to reinforce how accrued expenditures and obligations are to be reported.

Open Recommendation[12]

Our September 2009 bimonthly report identified a need for additional federal guidance in defining green jobs and we made the following recommendation to the Secretary of Labor:

---

[11]GAO-10-604, 244.

[12]GAO-09-1016, 78.

- To better support state and local efforts to provide youth with employment and training in green jobs, provide additional guidance about the nature of these jobs and the strategies that could be used to prepare youth for careers in green industries.

Agency Actions

Labor agreed with our recommendation and has begun to take several actions to implement it. Labor's Bureau of Labor Statistics has developed a definition of green jobs which was finalized and published in the *Federal Register* on September 21, 2010. In addition, Labor continues to host a Green Jobs Community of Practice, an online virtual community available to all interested parties. As part of this effort, in December 2010, Labor hosted its first Recovery Act Grantee Technical Assistance Institute, which focused on critical success factors for achieving the goals of the grants and sustaining the impact into the future. The department also hosted a symposium on April 28-29, 2011, with the green jobs state Labor Market Information Improvement grantees. Symposium participants shared recent research findings, including efforts to measure green jobs, occupations, and training in their states. In addition, the department released a new career exploration tool called "mynextmove" (www.mynextmove.gov) in February 2011. This Web site includes the Occupational Information Network (O*NET) green leaf symbol to highlight green occupations. Furthermore, Labor's implementation study of the Recovery Act-funded green jobs training grants is still ongoing. The interim report is expected in late 2011.

Executive Office of the President: Office of Management and Budget

Open Recommendation

To leverage Single Audits as an effective oversight tool for Recovery Act programs, we recommended that the Director of the Office of Management and Budget (OMB)

1. provide more direct focus on Recovery Act programs through the Single Audit to help ensure that smaller programs with higher risk have audit coverage in the area of internal controls and compliance;[13]

2. take additional efforts to provide more timely reporting on internal controls for Recovery Act programs for 2010 and beyond;[14]

3. evaluate options for providing relief related to audit requirements for low-risk programs to balance new audit responsibilities associated with the Recovery Act;[15]

4. issue Single Audit guidance in a timely manner so that auditors can efficiently plan their audit work;[16]

5. issue the OMB Circular No. A-133 Compliance Supplement no later than March 31 of each year;[17]

6. explore alternatives to help ensure that federal awarding agencies provide their management decisions on the corrective action plans in a timely manner;[18] and

7. shorten the timeframes required for issuing management decisions by federal agencies to grant recipients.[19]

Agency Actions

(1) To provide more direct focus on Recovery Act programs through the Single Audit to help ensure that smaller programs with higher risk have audit coverage in the area of internal controls and compliance, the OMB Circular No. A-133, Audits of States, Local Governments, and Non-Profit Organizations 2010 Compliance Supplement (Compliance Supplement) required all federal programs with expenditures of Recovery Act awards to be considered as programs with higher risk when performing standard

---

[13]GAO-09-829, 127.

[14]GAO-10-604, 247.

[15]GAO-09-829, 127.

[16]GAO-10-604, 247.

[17]GAO-10-999, 194.

[18]GAO-10-604, 247-248.

[19]GAO-10-999, 194.

risk-based tests for selecting programs to be audited.[20] The auditor's determination of the programs to be audited is based upon an evaluation of the risks of noncompliance occurring that could be material to an individual major program. The Compliance Supplement has been the primary mechanism that OMB has used to provide Recovery Act requirements and guidance to auditors.[21] One presumption underlying the guidance is that smaller programs with Recovery Act expenditures could be audited as major programs when using a risk-based audit approach. The most significant risks are associated with newer programs that may not yet have the internal controls and accounting systems in place to help ensure that Recovery Act funds are distributed and used in accordance with program regulations and objectives. Since Recovery Act spending is projected to continue through 2016, we believe that it is essential that OMB provide direction in Single Audit guidance to help to ensure that smaller programs with higher risk are not automatically excluded from receiving audit coverage based on their size and standard Single Audit Act requirements.

In May 2011, we spoke with OMB officials and reemphasized our concern that future Single Audit guidance provide instruction that helps to ensure that smaller programs with higher risk have audit coverage in the area of internal controls and compliance. OMB officials agreed and stated that such guidance is included in the 2011 Compliance Supplement which was to be issued by March 31, 2011. On June 1, 2011, OMB issued the 2011 Compliance Supplement which contains language regarding the higher-risk status of Recovery Act programs, requirements for separate reporting of findings, and a list of Recovery Act programs to aid the auditors. We will continue to monitor OMB's efforts to provide more direct focus on

---

[20]Congress passed the Single Audit Act, as amended, 31 U.S.C. ch. 75, to promote, among other things, sound financial management, including effective internal controls, with respect to federal awards administered by nonfederal entities. The Single Audit Act requires states, local governments, and nonprofit organizations expending $500,000 or more in federal awards in a year to obtain an audit in accordance with the requirements set forth in the act. A Single Audit consists of (1) an audit and opinions on the fair presentation of the financial statements and the Schedule of Expenditures of Federal Awards; (2) gaining an understanding of and testing internal control over financial reporting and the entity's compliance with laws, regulations, and contract or grant provisions that have a direct and material effect on certain federal programs (i.e., the program requirements); and (3) an audit and an opinion on compliance with applicable program requirements for certain federal programs.

[21]In addition to the annual edition of the Compliance Supplement, OMB may issue Compliance Supplement addendums during the year to update or provide further Recovery Act guidance.

Recovery Act programs through the Single Audit to help ensure that
smaller programs with higher risk have audit coverage in the area of
internal controls and compliance.

(2) To address the recommendation for taking additional efforts to
encourage more timely reporting on internal controls for Recovery Act
programs for 2010 and beyond, OMB commenced a second voluntary
Single Audit Internal Control Project (project) in August 2010 for states
that received Recovery Act funds in fiscal year 2010.[22] Fourteen states
volunteered to participate in the second project. One of the project's goals
is to achieve more timely communication of internal control deficiencies
for higher-risk Recovery Act programs so that corrective action can be
taken more quickly. Specifically, the project encourages participating
auditors to identify and communicate deficiencies in internal control to
program management 3 months sooner than the 9-month time frame
currently required under OMB Circular No. A-133. Auditors were to
communicate these through interim internal control reports by December
31, 2010. The project also requires that program management provide a
corrective action plan aimed at correcting any deficiencies 2 months
earlier than required under statute to the federal awarding agency. Upon
receiving the corrective action plan, the federal awarding agency has 90
days to provide a written decision to the cognizant federal agency for audit
detailing any concerns it may have with the plan. Each participating state
was to select a minimum of four Recovery Act programs for inclusion in
the project.

We assessed the results of the first OMB Single Audit Internal Control
Project for fiscal year 2009 and found that it was helpful in communicating
internal control deficiencies earlier than required under statute. We
reported that 16 states participated in the first project and that the states
selected at least two Recovery Act programs for the project. We also
reported that the project's dependence on voluntary participation limited
its scope and coverage and that voluntary participation may also bias the
project's results by excluding from analysis states or auditors with
practices that cannot accommodate the project's requirement for early
reporting of control deficiencies. Overall, we concluded that although the
project's coverage could have been more comprehensive, the analysis of

---

[22]OMB's second project is similar to its first Single Audit Internal Control project which
started in October 2009. Sixteen states participated in the first project. We assessed the
results of the project and reported them in GAO-10-999.

the project's results provided meaningful information to OMB for better oversight of the Recovery Act programs selected and information for making future improvements to the Single Audit guidance.

OMB's second Single Audit Internal Control Project is in progress and its planned completion date is June 2011. OMB plans to assess the project's results after its completion date. The 14 participating states have met the milestones for submitting interim internal control reports by December 31, 2010 and their corrective action plans by January 31, 2011. By April 30, 2011, the federal awarding agencies were to provide their interim management decisions to the cognizant agency for audit. We discussed the preliminary status of these interim management decisions with OMB officials and, as of May 24, 2011, only 1 of the 10 federal awarding agencies had submitted some management decisions on the auditees' corrective action plans as required by the project's guidelines. On May 24, 2011, officials from the cognizant agency for audit, HHS, reemphasized to the federal awarding agencies their responsibilities for providing management decisions in accordance with the project's due dates. In our review of the 2009 project, we noted similar concerns that federal awarding agencies submitted management decisions on proposed corrective actions in an untimely manner and made recommendations in this area, which are discussed later in this report. We will continue to monitor the status of OMB's efforts to implement this recommendation and believe that OMB needs to continue taking steps to encourage timelier reporting on internal controls through Single Audits for Recovery Act programs.

(3) We previously recommended that OMB evaluate options for providing relief related to audit requirements for low-risk programs to balance new audit responsibilities associated with the Recovery Act. OMB officials have stated that they are aware of the increase in workload for state auditors who perform Single Audits due to the additional funding to Recovery Act programs and corresponding increases in programs being subject to audit requirements. OMB officials stated that they solicited suggestions from state auditors to gain further insights to develop measures for providing audit relief. However, OMB has not yet put in place a viable alternative that would provide relief to all state auditors that conduct Single Audits. For state auditors that are participating in the second OMB Single Audit Internal Control Project, OMB has provided some audit relief by modifying the requirements under Circular No. A-133 to reduce the number of low-risk programs to be included in some project participants' risk assessment requirements.

OMB is taking initiatives to examine the Single Audit process. OMB officials have stated that they have created a workgroup which combines the Executive Order 13520—Reducing Improper Payments Section 4 (b) Single Audit Recommendations Workgroup (Single Audit Workgroup), and the Circular No. A-87—Cost Principles for State, Local, and Indian Tribal Governments Workgroup (Circular No. A-87 Workgroup). The Single Audit Workgroup is comprised of representatives from the federal audit community; federal agency management officials involved in overseeing the Single Audit process and programs subject to that process; representatives from the state audit community; and staff from OMB. OMB officials tasked the Single Audit Workgroup with developing recommendations to improve the effectiveness of Single Audits of nonfederal entities that expend federal funds in order to help identify and reduce improper payments. In June 2010, the Single Audit Workgroup developed recommendations, some of which are targeted toward providing audit relief to auditors who conduct audits of grantees and grants that are under the requirements of the Single Audit Act. OMB officials stated that the recommendations warrant further study and that the workgroup is continuing its work on the recommendations. OMB officials also stated that the Circular No. A-87 Workgroup has also made recommendations which could impact Single Audits and that the workgroups have been collaborating to ensure that the recommendations relating to Single Audit improvements are compatible and could improve the Single Audit process. The combined workgroups plan to issue a report to OMB by August 29, 2011. We will continue to monitor OMB's progress to achieve this objective.

(4) (5) With regard to issuing Single Audit guidance in a timely manner, and specifically the OMB Circular No. A-133 Compliance Supplement, we previously reported that OMB officials intended to issue the 2011 Compliance Supplement by March 31, 2011.[23] In December 2010, OMB provided to the American Institute of Certified Public Accounts (AICPA) a draft of the 2011 Compliance Supplement which the AICPA published on its Web site. In January 2011, OMB officials reported that the production of the 2011 Compliance Supplement was on schedule for issuance by March 31, 2011. OMB issued the 2011 Compliance Supplement on June 1, 2011. We spoke with OMB officials regarding the reasons for the delay of this important guidance to auditors. OMB officials stated that its efforts were

---

[23]The Compliance Supplement is updated annually. The 2010 Compliance Supplement was issued in July 2010 and is applicable to audits of fiscal years beginning after June 30, 2009.

refocused toward priorities relating to the expiration of several continuing resolutions[24] that temporarily funded the federal government for fiscal year 2011, and the Department Of Defense And Full-Year Continuing Appropriations Act, 2011, which was passed by the Congress in April 2011, averting a governmentwide shutdown. OMB officials stated that, as a result, although they had taken steps to issue the 2011 Compliance Supplement by the end of March, such as starting the process earlier in 2010 and giving agencies strict deadlines for program submissions, they were only able to issue it on June 1, 2011. We will continue to monitor OMB's progress to achieve this objective.

(6) (7) In October 2010, OMB officials stated that, based on their assessment of the results of the project, they had discussed alternatives for helping to ensure that federal awarding agencies provide their management decisions on the corrective action plans in a timely manner, including possibly shortening the time frames required for federal agencies to provide their management decisions to grant recipients.[25] However, OMB officials have yet to decide on the course of action that they will pursue to implement this recommendation. OMB officials acknowledged that the results of the 2009 OMB Single Audit Internal Control Project confirmed that this issue continues to be a challenge. They stated that they have met individually with several federal awarding agencies that were late in providing their management decisions in the 2009 project to discuss the measures that the agencies will take to improve the timeliness of their management decisions. Earlier in this report, we discussed that preliminary observations of the results of the second project have identified that several federal awarding agencies' management decisions on the corrective actions that were due April 30, 2011, have also not been issued in a timely manner.

---

[24]Continuing resolutions (also known as "CRs") are appropriations acts that provide budget authority for federal agencies, specific activities, or both to continue in operation when Congress and the President have not completed action on the regular appropriations acts by the beginning of the fiscal year. A CR may be enacted for the full year, up to a specified date, or until regular appropriations are enacted.

[25]The project's guidelines called for the federal awarding agencies to complete (1) performing a risk assessment of the internal control deficiency and identify those with the greatest risk to Recovery Act funding and (2) identifying corrective actions taken or planned by the auditee. OMB guidance requires this information to be included in a management decision that the federal agency was to have issued to the auditee's management, the auditor, and the cognizant agency for audit.

In March 2010, OMB issued guidance under memo M-10-14, item 7, (http://www.whitehouse.gov/sites/default/files/omb/assets/memoranda_20 10/m1014.pdf) that called for federal awarding agencies to review reports prepared by the Federal Audit Clearinghouse regarding Single Audit findings and submit summaries of the highest-risk audit findings by major Recovery Act program, as well as other relevant information on the federal awarding agency's actions regarding these areas. In May 2011, we reviewed selected reports prepared by federal awarding agencies that were titled *Use of Single Audit to Oversee Recipient's Recovery Act Funding*. These reports were required by memo M-10-14 for reports from the Federal Audit Clearinghouse for fiscal year 2009. The reports were developed for entities where the auditor issued a qualified, adverse, or disclaimer audit opinion. The reports identified items such as (1) significant risks to the respective program that was audited; (2) material weaknesses, instances of noncompliance, and audit findings that put the program at risk; (3) actions taken by the agency; and (4) actions planned by the agency. OMB officials have stated that they plan to use this information to identify trends that may require clarification or additional guidance in the Compliance Supplement.

OMB officials also stated that they are working on a metrics project with the Recovery Accountability and Transparency Board to develop metrics for determining how federal awarding agencies are to use information available in the Single Audit and which can serve as performance measures. We attended a presentation of the OMB Workgroup that is working with the Recovery Accountability and Transparency Board in developing the metrics project in May 2011 and note that it is making progress. OMB officials have stated that the metrics could be applied at the agency level, by program, to allow for analysis of Single Audit findings, along with other uses to be determined. One goal of the metrics project is to increase the effectiveness and timeliness of federal awarding agencies' actions to resolve single audit findings. We will continue to monitor the progress of these efforts to determine the extent that they improve the timeliness of federal agencies' actions to resolve audit findings so that risks to Recovery Act funds are reduced and internal controls in Recovery Act programs are strengthened.

Department of Transportation

Open Recommendations[26]

To ensure that Congress and the public have accurate information on the extent to which the goals of the Recovery Act are being met, we recommended that the Secretary of Transportation direct FHWA to take the following two actions:

- Develop additional rules and data checks in the Recovery Act Data System, so that these data will accurately identify contract milestones such as award dates and amounts, and provide guidance to states to revise existing contract data.

- Make publicly available—within 60 days after the September 30, 2010, obligation deadline—an accurate accounting and analysis of the extent to which states directed funds to economically distressed areas, including corrections to the data initially provided to Congress in December 2009.

Agency Actions

In its response, DOT stated that it implemented measures to further improve data quality in the Recovery Act Data System, including additional data quality checks, as well as providing states with additional training and guidance to improve the quality of data entered into the system. DOT also stated that as part of its efforts to respond to our draft September 2010 report in which we made this recommendation on economically distressed areas, it completed a comprehensive review of projects in these areas, which it provided to GAO for that report. DOT recently posted an accounting of the extent to which states directed Recovery Act transportation funds to projects located in economically distressed areas on its Web site, and we are in the process of assessing these data.

Open Recommendation[27]

To better understand the impact of Recovery Act investments in transportation, we believe that the Secretary of Transportation should ensure that the results of these projects are assessed and a determination made about whether these investments produced long-term benefits. Specifically, in the near term, we recommended that the Secretary direct FHWA and FTA to determine the types of data and performance measures

---

[26]GAO-10-999, 187-188.

[27]GAO-10-604, 241-242.

they would need to assess the impact of the Recovery Act and the specific authority they may need to collect data and report on these measures.

Agency Actions

In its response, DOT noted that it expected to be able to report on Recovery Act outputs, such as the miles of road paved, bridges repaired, and transit vehicles purchased, but not on outcomes, such as reductions in travel time, nor did it commit to assessing whether transportation investments produced long-term benefits. DOT further explained that limitations in its data systems, coupled with the magnitude of Recovery Act funds relative to overall annual federal investment in transportation, would make assessing the benefits of Recovery Act funds difficult. DOT indicated that, with these limitations in mind, it is examining its existing data availability and, as necessary, would seek additional data collection authority from Congress if it became apparent that such authority was needed. DOT plans to take some steps to assess its data needs, but it has not committed to assessing the long-term benefits of Recovery Act investments in transportation infrastructure. We are therefore keeping our recommendation on this matter open.

Matters for Congressional Consideration

Matter[28]

To the extent that appropriate adjustments to the Single Audit process are not accomplished under the current Single Audit structure, Congress should consider amending the Single Audit Act or enacting new legislation that provides for more timely internal control reporting, as well as audit coverage for smaller Recovery Act programs with high risk.

We continue to believe that Congress should consider changes related to the Single Audit process.

Matter[29]

To the extent that additional coverage is needed to achieve accountability over Recovery Act programs, Congress should consider mechanisms to provide additional resources to support those charged with carrying out the Single Audit Act and related audits.

[28]GAO-09-829, 128.

[29]GAO-09-829, 128.

We continue to believe that Congress should consider changes related to the Single Audit process.

Matter[30]

To provide housing finance agencies (HFA) with greater tools for enforcing program compliance, in the event the Section 1602 Program is extended for another year, Congress may want to consider directing the Department of the Treasury to permit HFAs the flexibility to disburse Section 1602 Program funds as interest-bearing loans that allow for repayment.

We continue to believe that Congress should consider directing the Department of the Treasury to permit HFAs the flexibility to disburse Section 1602 Program funds as interest-bearing loans that allow for repayment.

---

[30]GAO-10-604, 251.

Appendix III: GAO Contact and Staff Acknowledgments

GAO Contact	David C. Trimble, (202) 512-3841 or trimbled@gao.gov
Staff Acknowledgments	In addition to the individual named above, Susan Iott, Assistant Director; Tom Beall; Jillian Fasching; Sharon Hogan; Susan Iott; Thomas James; Yvonne Jones; Jonathan Kucskar; Kirsten Lauber; Carol Patey; Cheryl Peterson; Brenda Rabinowitz; Beverly Ross; Kelly Rubin; Carol Herrnstadt Shulman; Dawn Shorey; Kathryn Smith; Jonathan Stehle; Kiki Theodoropoulos; and Ethan Wozniak made key contributions to this report.